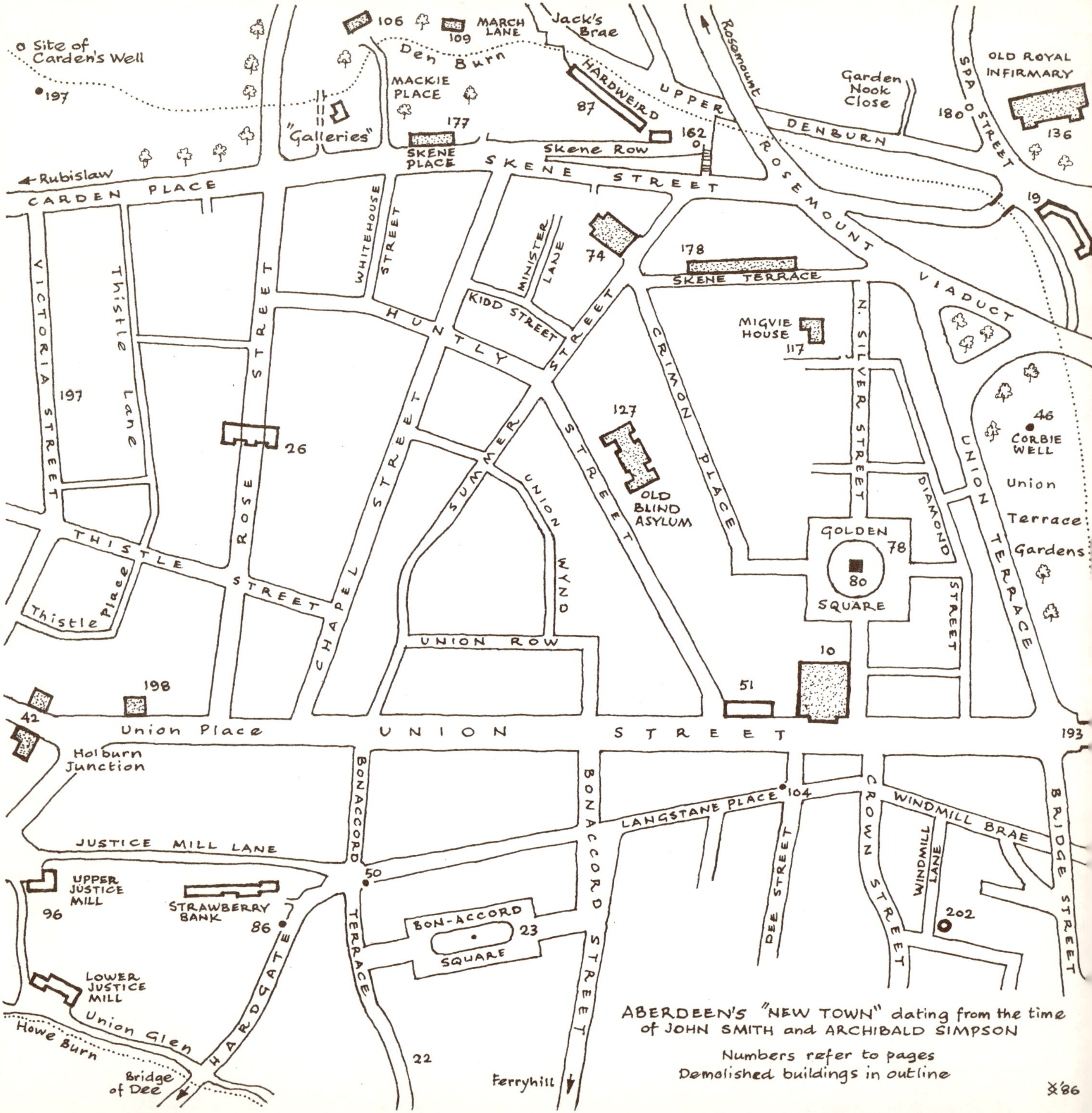

ABERDEEN'S "NEW TOWN" dating from the time of JOHN SMITH and ARCHIBALD SIMPSON

Numbers refer to pages

Demolished buildings in outline

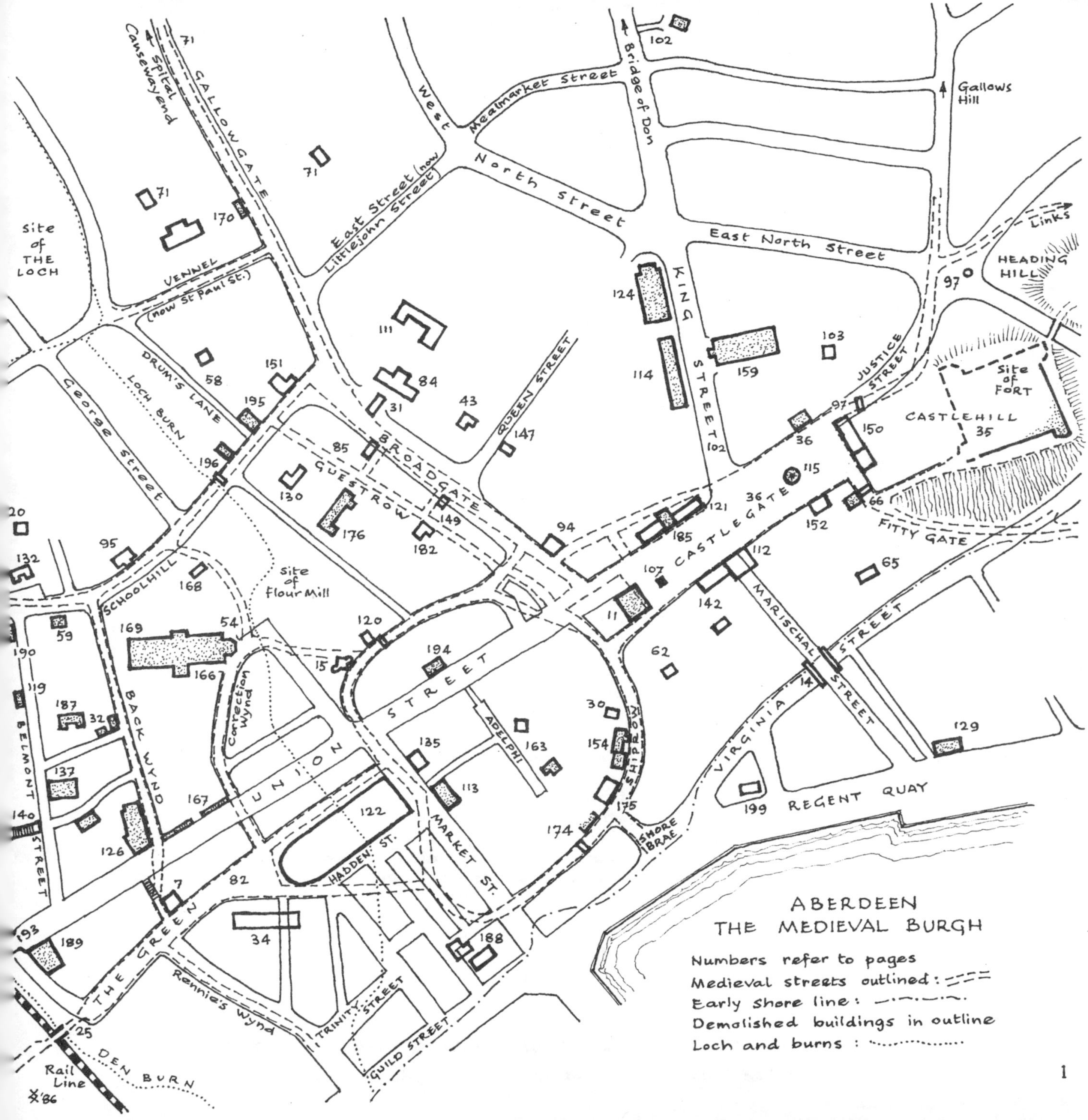
ABERDEEN
THE MEDIEVAL BURGH
Numbers refer to pages
Medieval streets outlined:
Early shore line:
Demolished buildings in outline
Loch and burns:
Spital
Canseway end
GALLOWGATE
West
Mealmarket Street
Bridge of Don
Gallows Hill
North Street
East North Street
East Street (now Littlejohn Street)
KING STREET
QUEEN STREET
Links
HEADING HILL
Site of FORT
CASTLEHILL
JUSTICE STREET
site of THE LOCH
VENNEL (now St Paul St.)
DRUM'S LANE
LOCH BURN
George Street
BROADGATE
GUESTROW
CASTLEGATE
FITTY GATE
SCHOOLHILL
Site of Flour Mill
MARISCHAL STREET
STREET
VIRGINIA STREET
REGENT QUAY
SHIPROW
SHORE BRAE
ADELPHI
Correction Wynd
UNION STREET
BACK WYND
BELMONT STREET
HADDEN ST.
MARKET ST.
THE GREEN
Rennie's Wynd
TRINITY STREET
GUILD STREET
DEN BURN
Rail Line
71
102
170
111
84
31
43
58
151
195
196
85
130
176
182
149
147
124
114
159
103
97
36
150
35
115
102
121
185
94
66
152
112
65
107
11
142
62
20
132
95
168
169
166
54
120
194
15
59
190
119
187
32
137
140
126
167
122
135
113
163
30
154
175
174
14
129
199
7
82
34
188
193
189
25
'86

Edward Meldrum D.Arch., F.S.A.Scot., was born in Aberdeen and is an Architect by profession; he has been involved in the preservation and restoration of historic buildings in North Scotland. A Past-President of Inverness Field Club, whose interests include Local History and Archaeology, he was also Chairman of the Architectural Heritage Society – Highland Group, whose aim is the study and protection of our Scots architecture. His other publications comprise of a series of guidebooks : "From Nairn to Loch Ness", "From Loch Ness to the Aird", "The Black Isle", and "Inverness"; also the folding map/guides: "The Cairns of Clava" and "Seeing Around Inverness".

ISBN 0 947 659 36 6

Published by

ABERDEEN AND NORTH EAST SCOTLAND FAMILY HISTORY SOCIETY.

· Printed by Rainbow Enterprises, Dyce, Aberdeen.

ABERDEEN OF OLD

Design, Drawings and Calligraphy by
Edward Meldrum

AN

·A·B·C·

•

ABERDEEN'S
ANTIQUITIES
ARCHAEOLOGY
AND
ARCHITECTURE
ARRANGED
ALPHABETICALLY

·Second Edition · 1987·

ABERDEEN OF OLD

The toun had then but ten short streets;
  To ilka hoose there was a yaird;
But these auld yairds grew sturdy reets
  An' ilka gate had aye its gaird.

The Don doon by the Braid Hill ran,
  The tide weesh up the Castle Brae;
An' where lang miles o' pier-wark stan'
  A half a score o' birlinns lay.

Where flowed the tide by Tarnty Mill
  The iron horse has noo his sta';
Frae Justice Port to Windmill Hill
  Was wavin' green wi' yairdins a'.

The Woo'manhill wis ae green knowe,
  An' up the Denburn's bonny bank
The Play Grun lay in Gilcolm's howe,
  The scene o' mony a merry prank.

. . . . .

William Forsyth

INTRODUCTION AND ACKNOWLEDGEMENTS

This book may not appeal to those who regard the past as an anathema, and by whom nostalgia is considered a disease. It is, nevertheless, the result of many years of study dating back to my days as an apprentice architect in the Aberdeen of some forty years ago.

The scope of the book is confined to within the bounds of the pre-1975 City and Royal Burgh, with one or two exceptions, and I have taken 1850 as the year dividing Aberdeen of old from modern times which arguably began with the advent of railways in the North East. Where only the site remains of a monument or building, the O.S. Map Reference numbers are given, omitting the initial letters NJ which apply throughout the area of the town.

It is assumed that interested readers will have some knowledge, not only of the topography of Aberdeen and the street layout, but also of the city's evolution from prehistoric times. Those not conversant with the general background of Scottish history and architecture are referred to the many excellent works by our national and local historians.

Much could be said about the continuing destruction – often unwarranted – of our heritage of good old buildings, with public and private developers equally to blame. Regrets are in vain after the fight has been lost, but the recent welcome increase in conservation pressure groups, and the new realisation that old properties are not necessarily uneconomic, indicates that, despite the so-called progressives who would ding it a' doon, history is decidedly not bunk, nor are aul' hooses junk. A.M.Davidson's poem (p.6) says clearly what the Abendonian-in-the-street thinks. Grateful acknowledgement is made for permission to publish his and the other poems.

While I accept responsibility for any speculative theories and for the inevitable errors of fact, my sincere gratitude is expressed to those who have helped me in various ways. In particular I acknowledge my great debt to the following who from my youth encouraged my interest in, and influenced my studies of, the history and antiquities of North East Scotland – Walter Humphries, Douglas Simpson, Fenton Wyness; and my father and mother, Adam and Christina Meldrum, to whose memory this book is dedicated.

VANDALISM

O fat hiv ye deen t' my ain native Toun,
for A'm fairly lost noo fan I stravaig aroon
an look for the streets far I played, a wee loon,
O fat hiv ye deen t' my ain native Toun?

Far's Strawberry Bank? Far's the auld Wallace Tour?
Fat's come owre the Denburn ablow and abeen?
An, dammit, ye've flittit oor Tarnty Ha',
rugged doon the New Market and muckt up the Green.

Far's the Northern Club wi its snod Coonty nobs;
an its hairmless neebor douce YMCA;
an fat's THAT ye hae biggit owre Union Brig
t' blin the wide vista owre-by Torry Bay?

They tell me some things are far better awa –
the Guestra' for een, forbye the Shipraw;
but fat are ye gyan t' plunk doon in their place –
a curn spunk boxes wi nae sowl, hert nor face.

An Ragg's Lane's awa, far we baitit the snout
fae Lodge Walk, fa's roch neive dealt mony a clout
fan we keekt roon the corner and roared "Tarry Hat!"
fyle the coorse heid abeen bared his teeth like a rat.

Och, A could rin on, but fat's the gweed
fan caul gless and concrete ye say's fat we need;
ye'll get yir ain wye A've nae doot, but, gweed Lord,
ye've fair made a sair soss o' MY Bon-Accord.

A.M. Davidson

Demolished in 1914, Aedie's House was characteristic of the old properties which once formed the Green. It stood - M.R. 94060612 - at the east corner of Aedie's or Addie's Wynd, the name of the steep brae at the south end of the old Back Wynd, known as the Wester Kirk-gate, or West Wynd, after it was laid out in 1594. About 1802, when Union Street was being built, the Back Wynd Stairs were erected – to be replaced by the present wider flights of steps in 1931.

Aedie's House had been built, possibly by the master-mason Andrew Jamesone (father of George Jamesone the artist), for Andrew Aedie, maltsman, who died 1604; his initials and those of Christian Guthrie his wife, were on one of the skewputts. The building, with its harled stone walls and steep pitched slated roof, had the rather unusual feature of a wide chamfer at the south-west corner between first floor level and eaves, where the skewputt was carried on three rounded corbel courses. Of the three storeys, there were latterly shops at pavement level, and at second floor were three fine dormer windows, added by David Aedie in 1633, which date, with his initials and coat-of-arms adorned the west dormer tympanum; that in the middle had a complex monogram of the initials D. Æ., and K.B. for his wife Kathren Burnet, and the eastmost bore the date 1633 and a shield carrying the combined heraldic arms of Aedie and Burnet. David Aedie was one of the many townsmen killed by Montrose's troops at the Battle of Aberdeen near the Justice Mills in 1644.

ALBERT STREET

Between Waverley Place and Carden Place is the attractive south part of Albert Street, named after the Prince Consort, husband of Queen Victoria. A residential "corridor" street, it was, like the adjoining Albert Terrace, designed by the architect, Archibald Simpson, in 1840 and carried out by Matthews and Mackenzie, Architects, after 1849, two years after Simpson's death. The east side (nos. 1 - 23) is of two storeys - a quite plain ashlar granite frontage with a flat band below parapet, pedimented dormers at attic level and the original iron railings above the basements. The west side (nos. 2-18) is single storey with attics and basements, the ground floor windows featuring cornices and consoles. The building of Albert Terrace - nos. 1-34 - was begun c. 1849; the south side was not complete till the 1870s.

Kenspeckle among the surrounding inter-war bungalow development of Ashley Gardens is this interesting piend-roofed two-storey mansion of late 18th century date, with later alterations including the over-large 19th century bow windows. The doorway has Tuscan pilasters and cornice. The house has the rough granite masonry exposed, but the walls had originally been harl-ed. Ashley was occupied by Patrick Davidson, Advocate, about 1840. In 1857 it was acquired by John Cook, Shipmaster, a descendant of a Craigievar family. The estate lay between Union Grove and Great West-ern Road. In the 1780s Friendship Farm stood where Ashley School and Friendship Terrace are now.

ASSEMBLY ROOMS

The Assembly Rooms, the first part of the Music Hall building, were built in 1820-Archibald Simpson (1790-1847), Architect. The style is Neo-Grecian, with a splendid portico of 6 high Ionic columns forming the main entrance facing on to Union Street. This dignified Classical building is the finest on Aberdeen's main thoroughfare; despite this, it was threatened with complete demolition in 1961.

The interior consists of an entrance vestibule and elegant foyer with Ionic columns and an elliptical domed ceiling. The Round Room has Corinthian columns and central oculus. The Square Room is domed and the Ballroom, with a segmental arched ceiling, was altered in the renovations of 1985.

The Concert Hall, fronting on to Golden Square, was added in 1858-9 - James Matthews, Architect.

First known as Union Buildings when designed in 1819 by Archibald Simpson, this became the Royal Athenaeum Hotel and Restaurant, a notable Georg-ian building forming a fine Classical terminal feature at the west end of the Castlegate at the corner with Union Street. It is four storeys in height and the arched ground floor doors and windows retain the original architectural design. At first floor facing the Castlegate is a central three windowed feature with four Ionic columns. At this level was the famous restaurant known, from 1888 on, as "Jimmy Hay's", a spacious high-ceilinged apartment with the estimable motto, on a freize round the four walls : "He that drinks well, sleeps well · He that sleeps well, works well · He that works well, eats well · He that eats well, drinks well." After being gutted by fire in 1973 the Athenaeum building was restored as offices five years later, unfortunately without including the restaurant once familiar to generations of convivial Aberdonians.

AUCHMULL HOUSE

This mansion house, plain and simple in its design occupied a commanding situation with views over to Persley and the valley and estuary of the River Don. The lands of Auchmull, originally part of the barony of Craibstone, became the property of James Gordon after 1547. About the mid-17th century the Alexander family became lairds, and Alexander Alexander was probably the builder of the house around 1750. By 1755 it was surrounded by plantations of half-a-million trees of various species and there were also herds of deer. Forestairs, horn-shaped in plan, led up to the entrance door; and the basement windows had chamfered surrounds. Front windows and doorway had raised architraves ; at wallhead level was a projecting eaves-tabling and curved skewputts terminated the plain gable skews. The basement kitchen had a 6ft. (1.8m.) wide chamfered arched fireplace.

Unroofed in 1953, the house was completely demolished by 1960, its site (M.R. 90240902) now occupied by Nos. 53-5 Heathryfold Circle.

Auchmill was the early 19th century name of the village now called Bucksburn, the name which in 1854 was given to the nearby station of the Great North of Scotland Railway.

This medieval earthwork – a Scheduled Ancient Monument – is sited in the east part (M.R.95750512) of the walled grounds of Balnagask House; in the 1950s it had a summerhouse on top. In the 12th century this was probably the "motte" castle of the De Nug (Nigg) family ; Cormac de Nug being referred to in a charter dated about 1180. The motehill stands around 8.5M. (28ft.) high, and the oval summit measures about 21M. (70ft.) north – south, and about 15M. (50ft.) east – west. It commanded the former ancient ferry-crossing at the mouth of the Dee, and formed the nucleus, with nearby St. Fittick's Kirk, of Nigg parish. Close by was the Mains – the medieval "desmesne" – a farm demolished in 1964. Nigg, the upland part of which was a deer-forest in the Middle Ages, was granted in 1233 by King Alexander 2nd to the Abbey of Arbroath. The wealthy Abbots certainly had a hall or "villa" at Balnagask around 1480, possibly on or near the site of the present House, into the west wall of which is built a panel with a very weathered coat-of-arms carved thereon. After the Reformation and during the 17th century, Balnagask was owned in turn by the Forbeses, Murrays and Menzies of Pitfodels.

Arbroath Abbey is recalled by local place-names such as Abbotswell, the site of the well – M.R.938039 – and later farm of that name being now built over with housing ; also the Spital Burn which joined the Dee south of Craiginches, its name apparently indicating a hospice, possibly with chapel, founded by the abbots for travellers crossing by an old ford, later replaced by the "Over-Ferrie" between Craiglug and Ferryhill.

BANNERMAN'S BRIG

Marischal Street was laid out in 1767 and its steep descent from the Castlegate to the harbour was mostly built up with terraced houses before 1790. The architect-mason for the upper portion was Archibald Simpson's uncle, William Dauney, who lived at No. 32, and who died around 1803. The three-storeyed stepped blocks have central doorways, some recessed with Roman Doric columns and good fanlights.

Halfway down, the street was carried across Virginia Street by "Bannerman's Bridge" – the earliest 'fly-over' in Scotland – a well proportioned single arch of 9M. (30ft.) span dating from 1768; William Law was the architect and Alexander Bannerman the builder. This attractive stone brig – a familiar landmark – was replaced in 1983 by a concrete bridge over the new roadway below, the widening involving demolition of Marischal Street blocks on the north side, Nos. 36-38, and No. 39 opposite. The flights of steps on the south side, leading down to Shore Lane, have been retained.

Below and behind the lower west side of the street, and running parallel, is the back close, Theatre Lane, so-called after Aberdeen's first theatre here; the Theatre Royal known as the "Band-box" opened in 1795 and closed in the 1870s.

Also known as the "Wallace Tower" or Well-house Neuk, Benholm's Tower or Lodging was demolished, with part of the Netherkirkgate, in 1964, despite the strongest pro-tests, to make way for a store. A large undistinguished structure replaced what had been not only a unique example of a Z-plan towerhouse within a Scots town but also one of the only four remaining 16th century buildings in Aberdeen. Built about 1588 by Sir Robert Keith of Benholm, brother of George Keith, 5th Earl Marischal, it stood - M.R. 94190628 - at the corner of Netherkirkgate and Carnegie's Brae or Putachieside. A picturesque land-mark typical of the best of our old burgh architecture its stone walls were originally white-harled, and though a little altered in the 1890s by conversion into a tavern it retained its corbelled stair turret, gun-loops, coat-of-arms panel, and the unusual but remarkable sculptured effigy of a knight in 16th century armour - possibly of Sir Robert Benholm the builder - in a deep recess above the string-course of the larger round tower; the other tower contained the entrance door and main spiral stair.

Although a replica building, incorporating some of the stonework and features of the demolished towerhouse, was erected in 1964 in Tillydrone Road, both the demolition and the pseudo-towerhouse showed serious lack of under-standing by the Scottish Office and the City Council of the real meaning and purpose of conservation of our historic buildings and their environment.

BISHOP'S GATE

This house – No.78 Don Street – is known as Bishop's Gate although it is on the other side of the street and a little way from the Bishop's Port or East Port. It is a two-storey building dating from the 17th century with later alterations and restoration. The windows are large with small panes and plain raised architraves; the fenestration is unusually unsymmetrical. Walls are harled save for the dressed work; there are no dormers on the steep-pitched slated roof.

Adjoining at the west gable, with its two wee attic windows, are four single-storey cottages along Clark's Lane – pleasantly neat in appearance under red-tiled roofs.

·Bishop's Lodging in 1950

No. 96 High Street is known as the Bishop's Lodging as there is a local tradition that this was the residence of one of the post-Reformation bishops of Aberdeen before 1688. The house was built in 1623, was demolished in 1950 and rebuilt two years later. The rebuilding was not a restoration as many of the unique original features were not replaced. The old house had harled granite walls, interesting fenestration on the street gable and wee dormers in the roof between ridge and eaves. The old double-leaf door had simple wrought-iron crook and band hinges. The door architraves were of dressed freestone and finely moulded, as were the dressed rybats, sills and lintels at window openings. Inside the house was a painted timber fireplace panel depicting fishers and their boats at a river-mouth; perhaps the work of some local artist. The chimney-copes are moulded, and the south-west skewputt was dated 1623 with the initials: M.I.K. and M.M. The former may refer to Master Johne Keith, recorded in the Oldmachar Session Accounts as Bursar of Divinity at King's College in 1642-3.

BISHOPS PALACE

Coat of Arms of William Gordon Bishop of Aberdeen at the Reformation.

The episcopal palace occupied the area - M.R. 940087 - just beyond the east wall of St. Machar's kirkyard, and over-looked to the north the Bishop's Ward - now Seaton Park. The Palace enclosed a large courtyard with towers at each of the four corners, with the hall and chambers of the bishop on one side, and the well in the middle. The entrance gateway was on the south side, another gate led to the Cathedral Kirk and a water-gate led towards the Don. The bishop's garden, which lay to the south-east between the court and the Chaplains' Chambers, had on its west wall a summerhouse, three storeys high. Next to the count was a close, from which was entered the bishop's green, surrounded by a dyke with a doocot on the north side. Within the green was the original site of the Sanctuary or Girth Cross. The Bishop's Port - demolished in the 17th century - was at the east end of the green and led to Seatongait, now Don Street.

Following the abandonment of the Bishop's castle on Tillydrone, the first episcopal residence here was in 1329, the builder being Alexander Kyninmond. In 1459 Bishop Thomas Spens rebuilt the Palace which stood as described above until in 1641 Principal William Guild of King's College had the great oak rafters of the bishop's hall cut down and removed to be built in at the College. Ten years later the Palace was demolished by the Cromwellian army and many stones were said to have been used to build the Fort on the Castlehill of Aberdeen.

The site is now built over with a students' residential hall, and during building operations in 1964 the facing stones of the bottom courses of the Palace walls were uncovered; investigation indicated three separate building periods.

Situated on the south side of Woolmanhill -M.R.93760638- this block of granite tenements, four and five storeys high, was built, the westmost house first, between 1798 and 1830, by James Black, wine merchant of Willowbank; his nickname locally was "The Black Prince". Although latterly run-down, neglected and marred by engine smoke from the adjoining railway, there was, despite their late date, a certain late medieval quality in these high buildings. The street frontage had interesting door fanlights, and the westmost basement was reached by stone steps with railings. The back (south) elevation was a good example of picturesque burgh architecture with lofty gables, stepped slated roofs topped by irregularly clustered chimney-heads, and a prominent projecting semi-circular stair tower. The whole block was demolished in 1957.

Beyond the west end of Black's Buildings at the foot of Skene Street, the Denburn during the early 19th century was crossed by Collie's Bridge, a stone structure built in 1802.

Blackfriars Street – 19th century tenements demolished c.1916

King Alexander 2nd is said to have gift-ed his house and gardens in Aberdeen to the Dominicans or Black Friars between 1230 and 1249. The lands of the Friary were bounded by the later streets of Woolmanhill, St. Andrew Street (formerly Hospital Row), Crooked Lane (which once skirted the Loch), Harriet Street and Schoolhill. Blackfriars Street was laid out at the end of the 18th century on what had been the Friars' gardens. It is believed that Gordon's College – the original Hospital block – with Gymnasium and swimming-pool, occupies the site of the conventual buildings and the chapel which was dedicated to St. John the Baptist, and later became the burial-place of the Keiths, Earls Marischal. The Friary grave-yard was apparently in the area – M.R. 939064 – between the Art Gallery and the MacRobert Hall; during the building of the former in 1885 a burial vault and human bones were uncovered. In 1503 the Friary had a Prior and thirteen friars. At the Reformation, in January 1560, the buildings were looted by the anti-Romist mob. In 1587 the whole of the property was granted to George Keith, 5th Earl Marischal. Some of the buildings, including the "manse of the Blackfriars", survived until the early 18th century.

According to a granite tablet inscribed with dates, the fort known as the Block House was erected in 1532 at Sand Ness, the sandy head--land now occupied by Fitty and the North Pier. It replaced an earlier fort, probably of timber dating from 1477. The Block House, stone-built, and intended for defence against pirates and English, was circular in plan with walling 6ft. (1.8M.) approximate thickness, pierced with gun-loops for cannons; a small caphouse, probably with internal stair to wallhead, was added about 1670. However in 1781 during the American War of Independence, two privateers, anchored in the estuary, were boarded and carried off by the notorious Capt. Fall, without any effective oppos--ition by the fort's artillery. By 1839, its defences abandoned, it became a smiddy. The building was finally removed in the 1870s, after which a fish-curing establishment, Nos. 14-18 Pocra Quay, was built in 1879 and a stone tablet set in the front wall. When this building was demolished in 1971, and the site developed by an oil company, the stone tablet was retained at pavement level.

Pocra was originally the Pockraw, meaning the fishing-net row, where nets or "pocks" were hung to dry. Pocra Quay was known as the New Pier when built pre-1773.

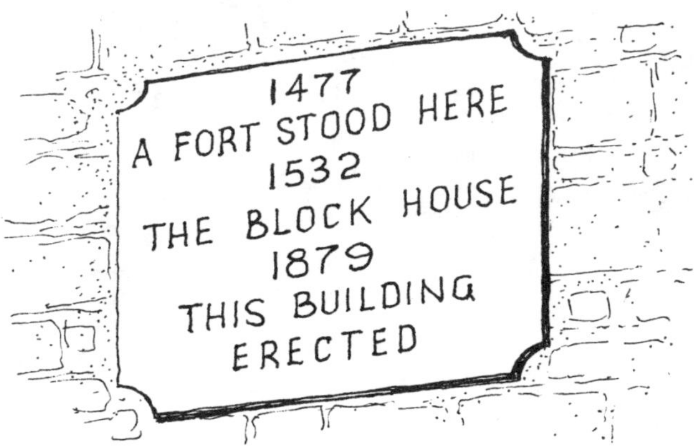

This fine crescent, with its splendid curve of light grey granite two-storey houses, Nos. 1-19, must have had a magnificent westward view, a century or so ago, overlooking the glen of the Howe Burn. It was begun like Bon Accord Square in 1823 to the design of the architect Archibald Simpson, on land belonging to the Incorporated Trade of Tailors. Most of the once-residential houses are now offices, clubs and hotels, and the sloping gardens opposite have been landscaped as park-land with trees and shrubs.

Nos. 1-17 and 2-20 Bon Accord Square, designed by Archibald Simpson to a rectangular plan with a central tree-clad garden, was begun in 1823; an example of formal townscape displaying appreciat--ion of frontage treatment on a gradual slope. The short approaches to the square from east and west – East and West Craibstone Streets – are also a part of the scheme, all the granite two-storey house facades being similar in scale and texture. All the properties were originally domestic, but have been converted to offices, clubs or hotels. Some houses in the south-east corner of the square have had small-paned windows restored, showing the initial fenestration effect.

Archibald Simpson died in 1847 at No. 1 East Craib--stone Street; in 1975 a memorial, in the shape of a simple block of grey granite was erected, to the memory of Simpson, in the middle of the open garden area of the Square.

BOTANY MANSE

No. 8 Chanonry on the west side of this old street is a stately Georgian building of two storeys built in granite ashlar with piended roof and central pediment. The attractive fanlighted front door is reached by an elegant railinged stair over the basement. The Botany Manse dates from the late 1700s, and the adjoining stone and brick walls are of the same era. This fine mansion occupies the site of two of the Cathedral's mediaeval manses : Ellon, which survived till the 18th century, and Cruden, which was demolished sometime after 1712.

Next door, No. 7 Chanonry is also of the late 18th century. A 3-storey house with attractive canopy over front door and steps, it has a piended and slated roof, and is built of granite rubble masonry with dressed work at doors and windows. This building occupies the site of the Parson of Deer's Manse, which was taken down around 1700.

This once-important landmark formed the link over the Denburn between Windmill Brae and the Green, and was thus the main entry to the early burgh. The brig was built of granite and consisted of one graceful arch, designed by local architect and builder John Jeans in 1747. Earlier timber bridges here were replaced by stone structures in 1556 and 1586, and by master-mason Andrew Jamesone's two-arched bridge, built 1609. This lasted until its demolition after damage due to spates in 1746. After the Denburn had been covered in, Jeans's Bow Brig was removed in 1851, and in its place a footbridge continued the old route over the railway, being enlarged into a thoroughly ugly iron bridge in 1910. This structure, locally called the "Puffin' Briggie" during the age of steam, was itself demolished in 1982. The pedestrian link from the Green to Windmill Brae has been retained within the Trinity Centre car park area. The only remaining parts of the Bow Brig of 1747 are one arch, 10.5M. (35ft.) wide, just visible under the arches of Union Terrace Gardens, laid out in 1877; and one granite lamp-post used to adorn the top of the rebuilt Corbie Well nearby.

· Bow Brig from the north around 1830

BRIDEWELL

The site of this building, which was known after 1842 as the West Prison was halfway - M.R. 933060 - along Rose Street from Union Street. Built in 1809 - Architect, James Burn of Haddington - the prison with its 109 cells was T-shaped in plan and four storeys high. The style was Castellated, with battlemented central and end towers five storeys high.

The Bridewell was closed in 1868, to be superseded by the East Prison, built in Lodge Walk in 1819. But its entrance gateways stood until 1883, being removed thereafter to allow the line of Rose Street to extend to Skene Street and Esslemont Avenue; the north half of Rose Street was originally called Henry Street after George Henry, Provost 1850-53.

While a bridge, probably of timber, existed over the River Dee in 1384, if not earlier, the Bridge of Dee is a seven-arched stone structure built, as dated, in 1520-5, the initiators of the scheme being Bishops William Elphinstone and Gavin Dunbar, the master-mason being Thomas Franche, with Alexander Galloway as master of work. The bridge is of granite construction, with sandstone for parapets and dressed work, including the many fine coat-of-arms panels, sculptured work and inscriptions. Repaired in 1718-21, the bridge was widened in 1841 by 3.3M (11 ft.) over the original width – John Smith, Architect. In 1545 a wooden gateway was built at the south end and was re-placed by a stone watch-house and Port, which was demolished in 1773. This fine bridge, the grandest in all Scotland in the 16th century, has particularly well-proportioned piers, with refuge cutwaters, and graceful ribbed arches; it is a Scheduled Ancient Monument.

At the north-east corner of the bridge, on a site marked by a few trees, stood the pre-Reformation Chapel of the Virgin Mary which had existed by 1530. It had contained a silver figurine known as Our Lady of Good Success, which disappeared during the chapel's destruction about 1560. This wee statue was later discovered in Europe, and has been since 1830 in the Church of Notre Dame de Finistere, Brussels.

BRIDGE OF DON

The "new" Bridge of Don, situated between the old Brig o' Balgownie and the Donmouth, carries the roadway to Ellon and Buchan. It was built between 1827 and 1830 by the contractor John Gibb to the designs of the City Architect, John Smith. These designs were done in collaboration with the famous bridge engineer Thomas Telford. The Bridge, of granite construction, does not have the spectacular aspect and beauty of setting of the Old Brig, but its five semi-circular arches are sturdy and graceful. The original width was 7.2M (24ft.) but in 1958 the widening of the Bridge to 19.8M (66ft.) between parapets allowed for a dual carriageway to cope with the increase in road traffic.

Downstream, in medieval times, the Don flowed southward in a channel through the Links to reach the sea near the Broad Hill. This watercourse, known as the "Old Don", was blocked in 1730 by a lengthy dyke of stonework and timber, designed and supervised by Professor James Gregory of King's College. Since then the river has flowed in an easterly direction to the sea. Above the bridge is a grassy island - Inch Allochy - opposite which on the north bank stood the now-demolished Don Mills - M.R. 94450955 - built as a distillery in 1798; vessels sailed up to the mill wharf before 1830.

Bridge of Don around 1950.

BRIG O' BALGOWNIE

This ancient and beautiful bridge, from medieval times till the early 19th century, carried the old north road out of Aberdeen. It spans the Don above the "Black Neuk Pot", the loveliest part of the picturesque lower reaches of the river. The Brig is a superbly well-proportioned single Gothic arch, and the building work was begun before the year 1290 by Richard Cementarius (the Mason), Provost of Aberdeen in 1272. His death in 1294 and the War of Independence probably caused an interruption in the work, and the bridge was completed around 1320 by Bishop Henry Cheyne on the order of King Robert the Bruce. Repaired about 1445, the structure was mostly rebuilt after 1605 when a mortification for the upkeep of the old "Brig o' Don" - its original name - was made by Sir Alexander Hay of Whitburgh. The bridge was causewayed in 1616, and repaired 1632; the buttresses on the east haunches were added about 1741, and further repairs done in the 1860s and '70s. Nowadays restricted to foot traffic the Brig - a Scheduled Ancient Monument - retains, with its neighbouring cottages, the attractive characteristic "old-world" atmosphere of past days.

ALEXANDER BURNETT'S LODGING

This was a "back-house" entered under the pend, at No. 40 Shiprow, of Jamieson's Court–M.R.94360624–on the north side of Provost Ross's House. A picturesque building, it was L-shaped in plan and three storeys high with a projecting corbelled-out stair turret. Its date was possibly 1634, as inscribed on a dormer pediment with the initials A.B. and I.C. Another stone, inscribed A.B. and 16.., partly indecipherable, had the combined coat-of-arms of the Burnetts – three holly leaves with a hunting horn, and the lion rampant, possibly for Crichton. This stone was removed from the house and built into a nearby boundary wall in the later 19th century. The house was probably built by Alexander Burnett, merchant, and a Baillie in 1650; his wife's name may have been Isabella Crichton. By 1939 Burnett's House, with the adjoining walls and other buildings on the west side of the upper part of the Shiprow had been swept away.

George Gordon Byron, later Lord Byron the poet, son of Catherine Gordon, last of the Gordons of Gight, and of Captain John Byron was born in London in 1788. His mother brought him to Aberdeen in 1790; after living at No. 10 Queen Street, they moved to this old Broadgate house, from which young Byron attended the Grammar School in Schoolhill until he left the town for England in 1798, when he became the 6th Lord Byron.
Byron's House at No. 68 Broadgate on the west side of the street - M. R. 94230644 - was interesting as a handsome example of Scots burgh architecture, until it was removed in 1902 - before the Marischal College facade was built. The house, dated about 1680, was three storeys high, the upper floor windows having very deep ogee-moulded surrounds. At eaves level was a corbel course with a high projecting skewputt at the south corner and a boldly corbelled-out turret under a fine bell-shaped slated roof.

One of the adjoining buildings to the north was the Waterhouse - also demolished 1902 - which was built in 1766 and contained a cistern supplied by springs at Fountainhall, Upper Gilcomston. A two-storey building with pedimented gable and clock facing the street, it ceased as a waterhouse in 1866.

MA CAMERON'S INN

Ma Cameron's before alteration.

In Little Belmont Street stands the most ancient and possibly also the most notable of Aberdeen's surviving aul' howffs, despite the alterations which have removed much of the inn's original unique interest and character. Particularly regrett-able was the replacement of the central chimney gable and steep-pitched roof by mansard-type dormers. Dating from about the end of the 18th century, it was for long a coaching inn. Unhappily the cobbled courtyard and old stabling at the back have been built over by the pub's bleak rear extension. Al-though the Cameron family were licensees for over 60 years from around 1870 till 1933, Mrs Mitchell, their successor with her husband, was often wrongly given the old "title" of Ma Cameron.

Next to the inn, on the corner, No. 2 Little Belmont Street is a sturdy three storey building with gable walls of coursed granite and the original curved skewputts, that at the north-east corner inscribed I.H. and 1787, evidently the date when built. The building, which had its original entrance door off Back Wynd, stands on the site of an earlier house, erected by the Professors of Marischal College, and demolished in 1772 to allow the junction of Little Belmont Street to Back Wynd.

First proposed in 1795, the canal was commenced the next year with Thomas Telford as consultant on design, and John Rennie as engineer. The waterway – 18¼ miles (29.4 Km.) long and 20ft (6M.) broad, with 18 locks – opened in 1807 for boat traffic between Port Elphinstone near Inverurie and Aberdeen harbour; the lock linking it to Waterloo Quay was not built until 1834. The basin here later became Waterloo goods depot after the canal, never a financial success, was bought in 1845 by the North of Scotland Railway Company. However the canal remained in use until 1854 when the railway – now disused – was laid out more or less along its route within the bounds of the city.

Street names such as Canal Terrace, Road and Street recall the old waterway, and one original small bridge remains at Station Road, Woodside – Map Ref. 922091. Other bridges, much altered and widened for railway traffic, but originally spanning the canal within the city are at Miller Street, Albion Street, Constitution Street, Park Street, King Street, Nelson Street, Mounthooly, Canal Terrace, Bedford Road and St Machar Drive, first known as Boat House Brae leading from the Aulton.

Old Canal Bridge · Station Road

CARMELITE FRIARY

The buildings of the Carmelite or White Friars occupied the area bounded by what are now Rennie's Wynd on the west, Trinity Street on the south, the Green on the north, and on the east Carmelite Lane, near the line of the old Flourmill or Malt-mill Burn. The Friary was founded some time before 1273, when Reginald le Chen made a grant to the Carmelites. The church, dedicated to St John, was completed by the middle of the 13th century. In 1980-1 excavations, just west of Martin's Lane - M.R. 94110609 - revealed foundations of the church buttresses and wall footings, and also some evidence of a cloister: many burials were un--covered, also decorated glass and pottery. At least four friars were in occupation at the Reformation before the destruction of the friary by the Protest--ants in 1560; later the lands were granted by King James 6th in 1583 to the Burgh Council. By 1647 only a piece of vaulting, the "Friars' Kiln", remain--ed of the buildings and although the whole area was built over, the semi-circular base courses of sand-stone walls, with splayed window openings, in the basement of No 6 Trinity Street - M.R. 94160604 - may now be the only visible masonry remains of the Friary. Nearby in Carmelite Lane, digging operations in 1891 uncovered a quantity of bones, perhaps in-dicating the location of the Carmelites' burial ground, which in 1648 was still existing, enclosed by a dyke to prevent flooding. In 1794 Carmelite Street was formed on ground which had been the Friary garden. The Carmelites are believed to have operated, from around 1400, a pottery on their lands of Clayhills, between the Den and Mill Burns.

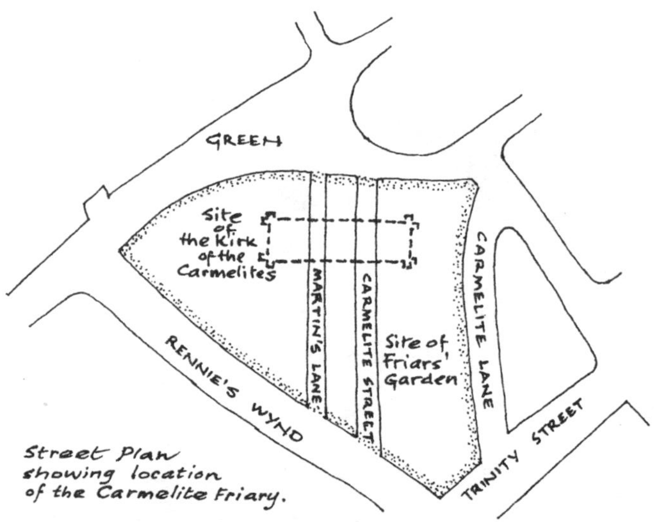

Street Plan showing location of the Carmelite Friary.

Cromwellian Fort – S.-E. bastion

Aberdeen's Royal Castle – dating like the burgh from around 1150 when David Ist was King – occupied the Castlehill and the Heading Hill to east of the Castlegait. Originally a timber and earthwork castle of the motte-and-bailey type, it dominated from its prominent situation – M.R. 94650640 – not only the Royal Burgh, but also the Dee estuary and harbour, and the coast beyond the Links. Its initial purpose was to protect burgh and port from Norse attacks and other dangers; it was strengthened in 1264, probably with stone defences – Richard Cementarius, mason – to resist possible English invasion. After its capitulation to the English in 1290, it was again surrendered in 1296, after which William Wallace's forces are said to have attempted its recapture. In the summer of 1308 King Robert 1st, aided by the Aberdonians, finally ousted and killed the English garrison. As Bruce's policy was to destroy all but the principal castles of his kingdom to prevent their re-fortification by the enemy, Aberdeen Castle was rased in this way and the Castlehill reduced in height. However some form of fortalice did exist until the 15th century, and the Kennedys of Kermuck held the office of Constable of Aberdeen Castle till 1669. The old chapel of St. Ninian (perhaps founded in the 5th or 6th century) stood on the Castlehill until the mid-16th century. On the Heading Hill – the bailey – Justice was dispensed, and here witch-burnings took place into the 17th century.

The Castlehill was fortified by General Monk's army during their occupation of the town in the 1650s, and within the walls of this Fort a military barracks was built in 1794-6. These buildings became slum tenements after 1935 and were demolished in 1965, after which this historic site was built over with flats of a mediocre design unfitting in such an important setting.

The only surviving portions of the Cromwellian Fort (dated 1651-2) are the south-east pentagon-shaped rubble-built bastion and the adjoining walls on the east and south, the Fort having been laid out to a simple rectangular plan, bastions at each corner.

Also called Castle Street, this "place" was originally the gait (way) to the Castle; it was the main square of the medieval burgh. Its other early name "Marketgate" indicates it was the market place from at least the 14th century. Of the remaining 18th century houses, several still stand on the north and south sides. Between the King Street corner and Justice Street, east of the arched pend of Bremner's Court (No. 9) are two 3-storey late 18th century tenements above shops — Nos. 10-11 and 15 — with Mathieson's Court the pend between. No. 16 is also 18th century originally four storeys with moulded granite skewputts. The finest, most interesting building is No. 17, dating from about 1760, a public-house known for more than a century before 1950 as "The Edinburgh Ale Establishment". Two-storeys in height, with heavy moulded eaves cornice, and lead box-gutters and downpipes, and raised framed window openings, the frontage includes the pend to Albion Court (No. 18) with its finely moulded round arch and jambs. The most well-known of the Castlegate's closes was Peacock's Close - now quite derelict.

On the south side, east of Marischal Street were National Bank Court (No. 42) and Pirie's Court (No. 50). The corner building is the large three-storey house, Nos. 51-54, with a symmetrical frontage emphasised by a centre chimney gablet containing two wee windows. Dated 1763 with initials I.F. on the corner skewputt, the house was built in coursed granite from the first granite quarry at Loanhead, opened 1730. The wide gable has a heavy projecting moulding at eaves height with an arched window above, under the very broad chimney.

No. 17 Castle Street.

The Chancellor of the Bishop's Chapter was also the Parson of Birse, and his Manse stood at the n.e. corner of the Chanonry (No. 16). In 1557 Alexander Seton the Chancellor disposed of it to George Seton, son of the Laird of Meldrum, and thereafter it passed to the Earl of Dunfermline, to Commissary John Scougal, and eventually to the Buchans of Cairnbulg who may have rebuilt and extended the old house in the early 18th century. At the end of the 19th century, Leslie of Fetternear, then owner, had it partially demolished, and the site is now occupied by a pleasing house of red sandstone, built 1935 – A.G.R. Mackenzie, Architect; this building includes older stones and a skewputt dated 1706, perhaps the date of rebuilding. The present outer wall is actually the lower part of the north and east walls of the 16th century manse with the original fine roll-moulded doorway, now a gate, and above it a barred window opening, containing a carved sandstone finial.

Chancellor's Manse in the 19th century.

To the west is Nº 15, Castleton House, erected about 1780 upon the site of the Chantor's House (Parsonage of Auchterless). The site of the Dean's Manse is now occupied by Nos. 14-14A Chanonry – partly 18th century with curved skewputts and moulded chimney copes. The Dean of the Chapter was also Rector of the Kirkton of Seaton.

Tillydrone House

The Chanonry of Old Aberdeen lies south of St. Machar's Cathedral, and within its precinct in the Middle Ages were the Manses of the Prebends of the Cathedral. The street now called Chanonry was originally the Chanonry-gait. None of the pre-Reformation manses remain but some of their sites are now built over by 18th and 19th century houses, several notable for their architectural merit.

Chanonry Lodge, Nº 13, a large late 18th century mansion with later work of around 1830, occupies the site of two medieval manses, that of the parson of Belhelvie and that of the Treasurer, the parson of Daviot. On the north-west of the Chanonry are three good Georgian houses : No. 10, where stood the Oyne manse, is a two-storey late 18th century residence; No. 11 is early 19th century with alterations of 1887, occupying the site of the Archdeacon's Manse (Parson of Rayne); Tillydrone House - 1820, John Smith, Architect - is an attractive one-storey house with basement and bow-fronted central entrance door. Here stood two manses, that of Mortlach and that of Kinkell, fronting what is now Tillydrone Road.

The south port, or gateway to the Chanonry-gait from the High Street was situated - M.R. 93900849 - just north-west of the Town House. It was also known as "Cluny's Port" after about 1623 when Sir Alexander Gordon of Cluny enclosed the gardens of the Manses of Invernochty (Strathdon) and Turriff and built a gallery and chamber over the port. Above the gate were some panels, including effigies of the Virgin - removed after the Reformation - and the Latin inscription :

"Hac ne vade via nisi dixaris Ave Maria
Invenies veniam sic salutando Mariam."

meaning : "Pass not this way unless you say Hail Mary
By such respect to Mary you will obtain pardon."

Another panel - the Old Aberdeen coat-of-arms, the pot of lilies - can still be seen ; now above the Town House door. The Chanonry Port was cleared away around 1790. Cluny's or Loch Wynd which led from the gate to the Dean's Loch (drained some time before 1782), where Cluny had an island summer-house, was absorbed in the road-widening and formation of St Machar Drive in 1924. This street-widening involved setting back the high wall, originally enclosing the Chanonry precinct, which dated from the 16th and 17th centuries, and is now the boundary of the Botanic Garden. Of the houses of the old wynd only No. 60 St Machar Drive - "Cluny's Port", so named because near its site, remains. Dated about 1770 it is interesting in that the lower walls are coursed granite rubble with cherry-cocking at joints, while the later upper walls are a contrast in red brick, Scotch-bond construction, from the local Seaton brickworks.

"Cluny's Port"

CHANONRY WELL

This simple yet handsome old well at the Cathedral Gate dates from about 1773 and is typical of the street wells once common throughout the Aulton; a similar well once stood outside the old Seaton-gait (Don Street) cottages. It is 3.3M (11ft.) high and built of ashlar granite with pyramid-al top and ball finial.

The Chaplainry Well stood near Chaplains' Court on the east corner - M.R.94060864 - of the Chanonry and Don Street; it disappeared in 1888. Another well of the same type stood in College Bounds and yet another in High Street.

Well at Cathedral Gate

CHAPLAINS COURT

The oldest house in Aberdeen, although altered internally in the 17th century and added to in 1718, dates from about 1519 when it was built by Bishop Gavin Dun-bar, whose coat-of-arms is above the roll-moulded arched pend (now built-up) which led to the Chap-lains' Chambers round a square courtyard, the south-west side of which was formed by this house. Three storeys high, the walls are partly rubble and partly ashlar with coped chimneys and corbie-step gables. The main house roof is of slates, while the wings are partly roofed with pantiles.

The Court - No. 20 Chanonry - had adjoining it the Chaplains' Port - M.R. 94060874 - which was the entry gate to the Chanonry from Seaton-gait (now Don Street). Removed in 1764 it had been erected between 1532 and 1545 by Bishop William Stewart, Chancellor of Scotland; it bore his name and also statues of the Virgin Mary, which were removed at the Reformation.

CHRIST'S COLLEGE

The tower of Christ's College is a dominant architectural landmark at Holburn Junction - or "Babbie Law's" - and is Union Street's west end terminal feature. Originally built as the Divinity Hall of the Free Kirk, it was erected in 1850 - Thomas MacKenzie, Architect. A two-storey building with high clock tower, it is designed in Tudor Gothic style, with coursed granite walls and dressed work at jambs and stringcourses, surmounted by a crenellated parapet. It now forms part of the University of Aberdeen.

Designed in a complementary style is the Library and Chapel (1887) on the opposite side of Alford Place; the architect was A. Marshall Mackenzie. This single-storey Gothic-style building, with its elaborate dormer windows behind the eaves-level balustrading, contains a fine long library room with a timber rib-arched ceiling. Professor William Robertson Smith held the Chair of Hebrew at this Free Kirk College from 1870 until his controversial dismissal in 1881.

This mid-17th century lodging stood where the present Greyfriars Kirk now is - M.R. 94290644 - and was at the head of Jopp's Court, the first close up old Broad Street beyond Queen Street. These properties were all demolished just after 1901 when the new frontage of Marischal College was being built. Of considerable architectural merit, Patrick Christie's House stood five storeys high, being L-shaped in plan with a square stair tower, and in the angle an upper stair turret with a conical roof. One skewputt had the initials P.C. for Patrick Christie, a merchant of the burgh who received a grant of armorial bearings in 1672. The entrance door at the base of the tower had above it an empty coat-of-arms panel. At the roof were corbie-stepped skews and boldly projecting spurstones, one initialled as above mentioned and with the coat-of-arms of Christie and Milne, evidently his wife's name. The original courtyard of this house was curtailed by the formation of Queen Street in 1775.

College Bounds
Old Gateway to Snow Kirk on left.

In this old thoroughfare, the south approach to the University precincts, two (formerly three) late 18th century two-storey houses on the west side have been sympathetically and pleasing-ly restored. No. 23 has two dormers with plain stone pediments, while No. 27, slightly earlier in date, has green-ish slates; both roofs have stone ridge tiling.
No 2, the first house on the east side of the Bounds is also late 18th century in date; it has a classical frontage and the entrance doorway has a small attractive canopy.

This two-storey house - No. 1 High Street - at the corner of Meston Walk has been modernised, the entrance door having been originally a pend. On the door lintel is the name "College Place" and above this is an unique small private insurance company sign - a gilt sun - dating from the early 19th century. The building itself dates from around 1800; the stone walls are of coursed granite, the chimney copes are plain brickwork, and door lintel and jambs have chamfered arrises.

Next door, No. 5, is of late 18th century date, also two-storeyed with rubble built granite walls. Neither house has roof dormers.

· College Place – Nº 1 High Street

· On right, Duncan's Place, now demolished.

CORBIE WELL

Corbie Well about 1940.

Supplied by a chalybeate spring, producing cool mineral water, this well existed before the 18th century. Moved from its original site – Map Ref. 938061 – in Union Terrace Gardens about 100 yards (30M.) to the south, the older well was replaced in 1898 by an outlet in a plain granite ashlar wall. An inscription-"Renewed 1856"-from the old well was removed during later modernisation, and until the 1960s the wall supported one of the stone pillar lamp-posts from the 1747 Bow Brig surmounted by the weather-vane from the steeple of old St. Nicholas Kirk.

Corbie Heugh was the name – because rooks nested there – of the brae above the Gardens. Near the original Corbie Well steps led up to the south end of Denburn Terrace and to the lower part of Skene Terrace, which, along with the iron foot-bridge over the now underground Denburn to Mutton Brae and Schoolhill, were cleared away by 1888, prior to the construction of Rosemount Viaduct and the north end of Union Terrace.

Known as Cotton Cottage around 1832, this was a charming one-storey house situated, before its demolition in 1960, in what is now Primrosehill Place - M.R. 927085. It had harled walls on a base of exposed masonry, and the eaves course and window surrounds were of dressed work; the low-pitch piend-ended roof was slated. There was a back basement. The most interesting architectural feature was the semi-circular, flat-roofed front entrance porch with its pilasters and Tuscan columns. The estate of Cot-toun or Cotton belonged to the Sandilands, who were a Jacobite family, from about the mid-1700s; by about 1775 James Jopp, five times Provost of Aberdeen between 1768 and 1786, became the owner. A wealthy merchant, as Provost he welcomed Samuel Johnson to the town in 1773, when the Doctor received the freedom of the burgh. Around 1780 Provost Jopp built the Lodge which on his death (1791) passed to his son until 1797, after which it had several owners, including Patrick Pirie of Gordons Mills in 1840.

Overlooking the River Don and Balgownie Brig this pleasant terraced group of wee cottages with their small windows, red pantiled roofs and little front gardens add considerably to the "old-world" character of this beauty spot. The most interesting are Nos. 9-20 Bridge Terrace and the oldest cottages are of early 17th century date. The one-storey building nearest the Brig was known as the Black Neuk Alehouse in the 18th century; the Black Neuk Brae climbed up the steep bank to Balgownie Road, the line of the old north road leading by Scotstown and Bishops' Loch. All the cottages were becoming ruinous and uninhabited by the middle of this century, and the group was completely restored - only the original walls and gables being retained - in 1959-60.

The Battle of the Bridge of Dee - or the first Battle of Aberdeen - was fought on 18th June 1639 between the Royalist army and the Covenanters, then led by Montrose, whose encampment was on the slope known as Covenanters' Faulds - M.R. 931034 - below Braeside farmhouse, demolished 1951. The housing scheme streets named after this historic site are some 400M. (¼ mile) away to the n.e. The bridge and its port, with its arched gateway and watch-tower chamber above, were defended by Viscount Aboyne's Royalist troops including several citizens of Aberdeen. The Covenanters eventually forced a crossing of the bridge and four Aberdonians were slain in the fighting. Some cannon-balls fired by the Royalists' four brass cannons were turned up by the plough when the Faulds area became farm parks, all now built over.

Covenanters Faulds around 1920

CRAB STANE

East and West Craibstone Streets take their name from the Crab or Craib Stane, situated at the s.e. corner of Langstane Place and Bon-Accord Terrace. The stone is traditionally linked to an Aberdeen merchant family descended from the 14th century baillie John Crab who was of Flemish origin and had connections with Berwick; it was probably a march stone of their Crabstone Croft. Moved to its present position when Langstane Place was widened the stone is a short block of light red granite about 29 ins. (735mm) high and 21 ins. (530mm) wide, with above it a bronze tablet and inscription set up in 1956.
Near here in 1571 occurred the Battle of the Crabstone, a clan fight in which the Gordons under Adam Gordon of Auchindoun defeated the Forbeses, capturing John, Master of Forbes.

This fine building, No. 204 Union Street, situated on the east corner of Huntly Street, was for over 150 years one of the most attractive buildings of real architectural merit on Aberdeen's main thoroughfare. Built in 1810 it was designed for Peter Milne of Crimonmogate by John Smith, Architect, (1781-1852). The facade had a slightly projecting centre bay with decorative oval window in the pediment which was flanked by ornate stone urns on the parapet above the dentilled cornice. Smith's main building consisting of basement, two floors and an attic, had a round archway on each side; later these were replaced by one-storey piend-roofed pavilion wings with a three-windowed Tuscan columned frontage. Four columns of the same order support the canopy of the main entrance to the house, which by 1840 had become the town residence of Sir Charles Bannerman of Crimonmogate; a derivative name is Crimond Place to the north of the property, which before 1955 was the premises of the Royal Northern Club. Demolished in 1963, this distinguished building was replaced by an ugly shopping block.

CROSS OF SEATON

This small Pictish cross-stone, about 900mm.(34 ins.) high by 600mm (23ins.) wide is probably of 5th or 6th century date; it is an undressed boulder with the incised carving of a simple cross with tenoned shaft. It may have been a boundary marker of early church lands but it was discovered - M.R. 94050932 - as part of "Seaton's Dyke" opposite Hill-head of Seaton. Into this dyke were built some carved stones from the Cathedral of St Machar, where, after the fall of the central tower in 1688, the east end became a source for building stone. This early cross may possibly date from the Dark-Age church, founded by St. Machar at Kirkton of Seaton, later to become the Cathedral Kirk. It now stands just outside the apsidal east end of King's College Chapel, but would be much more appropriately located within the Cathedral.

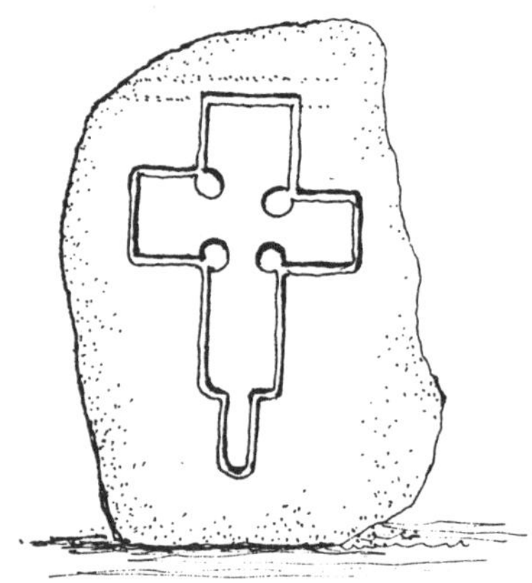

Built on solid rock on the south bank of the Don near the Brig o' Balgownie, this notable 17th century building - also known as the Chapter House - was in 1973 carefully restored as a residence by Aberdeen City Council. The L-plan house is of two floors, the walls of rough granite are harled, and the chamfered window surrounds are of sandstone. Leading into a pleasant garden court is a round-arched moulded sandstone gateway with a fine coat-of-arms panel bearing the shield of George Cruickshank of Berriehill, who was Dean of Guild 1664-6, and of Barbara Hervie his first wife, who died in childbirth 1669; with their initials: B. G. C. H. and the date 1655, indicating either their marriage date or when the house was completed. Carved skewputts at eaves have the date 1653, when the house was probably started, and also the same initials as above, those on the s.e. spurstone being carved in an elaborate monogram.

Other interesting houses at the south end of the Brig are Nos. 1 and 2 Rocky Bank dating from 1722; the late 18th century Brig House; and Rose Cottage and Brig End built in the early 1800s.

CRYPT CHAPEL

Under the east end and apse of St Nicholas East Kirk is this excellent example of Scots Gothic church architecture, the rib and groin vaulted crypt chapel dedicated to the Virgin Our Lady of Pity by the founder Lady Elizabeth Gordon, heiress of the Gordons of Huntly; her burial place is here. Still a place of worship, the chapel dates from before 1438, the architect being John Gray, the master-mason Richard Ancram; the master of works is believed to have been Sir Andrew Wricht. The exterior stonework was refaced in 1837 – Archibald Simpson, Architect, and the interior restored in 1898. The vaults of the central chapel, replastered 1977, retain the original structure of groined ribs rising from grotesquely carved corbels to the wooden boss with the initials MA for Maria. In the aisles the centre bosses depict armorial bearings and the legend of St. Nicholas. Both chapel and adjoining vestry contain some beautiful pre-Reformation carved woodwork, particularly the desk incorporating panels from choir stalls, carved by John Fendour the Aberdeen wright who lived around 1510; and the black oaken screen with the earliest known reproduction of the burgh's coat-of-arms, with date 1606 and the name and armorial bearings of Provost Alexander Rutherford of Rubislaw.

Now Nos. 12-14 Devanha Gardens, this house was built in 1813 for William Black, owner of the once-famous and now demolished Devanha Brewery, sited on the riverside. Extended (1840) by Archibald Simpson, it is of two storeys with sunk basement. Walls are of painted stucco with granite base course; the entrance porch has four fluted Greek Doric columns and the bow ends at east and west have Tuscan pilasters up to eaves height while the south bow has an attractive trellis veranda. This notable example of Georgian design was owned by James Blaikie around 1840; this family produced two Provosts, James Blaikie in 1833-5, and Sir Thomas Blaikie in 1839-46, and in 1853-5.

DOWER HOUSE

No. 55 Don Street is known as the "Dower House" because it was the residence of the Lady of Grandholm, the daughter of Mackenzie of Ardross and wife of John Paton of Grandholm a noted Jacobite during the 1715 Rising. It is now one house formed of two; the three-storey part was originally No. 53 where the old door is now built up. The two lower storeys have coursed granite walls; the upper part has uncoursed stone-work, a later addition. The windows have the original chamfered arrises and are small-paned. Of the two curved skewputts on the street elevation, that at the south-west corner is inscribed with the date 1770 and the initials A.H. The entrance to the house is in the adjoining two-storey part which has uncoursed granite walls and is of later date. In the back garden is a stone dated 1690, probably from the building to the west, now demolished. The adjoining boundary wall to the Chanonry, of granite rubble later heightened by brickwork, is of 17th and 18th century date. Restoration of the Dower House was carried out in 1984 — Oliver Humphries, Architect.

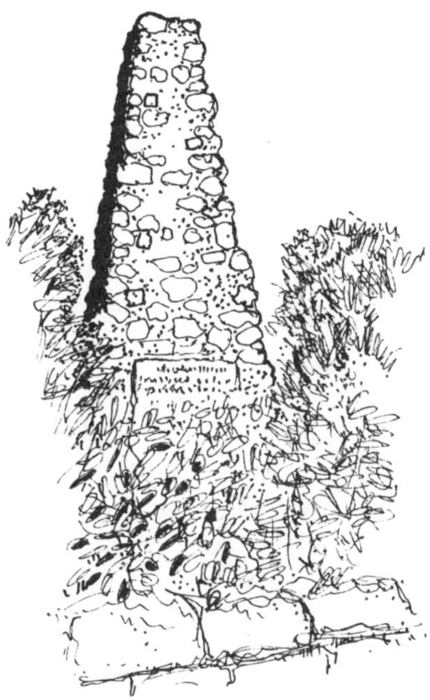

On the corner of Tillydrone Road and Avenue is a small obelisk-type of monument - M.R. 93530891 - about 2·7M. (9 ft.) high, built of reddish granite rubble blocks above a dressed stone plinth. The inscription indicates its association with the legend of the death - by heart failure presumably, after a mock trial by students - of George Downie or Dauney, the University's Sacrist in the 18th century; however no sacrist of that name is in the records. The "cairn" possibly originated as one of the follies in the late 18th century landscape garden of Berryden. It was moved to its present site in 1926, having till then stood on a low mound near where the Northern Co-operative Society's buildings are today, east of Berryden Road. Downie's Hows was the name, around 1790, of low ground near Back Hilton Road north of what was then called Belmont. This howe was traditionally believed to have been the sacrist's burial place but the place-name may derive from Gaelic dunan - "hillock".

Drum's Lane was formed in 1800 from garden ground originally part of Lady Drum's Hospital – site: M.R. 94130645 – which Lady Marian Douglas, wife of Sir Alexander Irvine of Drum, endowed (1633) for poor widows and spinsters.

On the south side of this lane – M.R. 94110647 – stood two houses (Nos. 5–7), late 18th century in date, which had Adam-type doorways with semi-circular fanlights. Front walls were exposed brickwork; dressed jambs, lintels and sills were granite; rainwater heads were finely executed in ornamental leadwork. These were demolished when the area was cleared in 1977. Also demolished was the Boys' Hospital, situated – M.R. 94110649 – on the north side of the lane; it gave its name to Boys Hospital Court from Upperkirkgate. This building began as the town house of Patrick Anderson of Bourtie and his wife Elizabeth Ogilvie; two skewputts were inscribed: P.A. B E.O. with the date 1741 when the house was built.
An incised panel had the initials and date: A.A. 1789, referring to Alexander Anderson, whose heirs rouped the property in 1828. The house – No. 42 St Paul Street – was a plain 3-storey building with a later semi-circular projecting wing on the west side; it accommodated the Boys' Hospital, an orphanage, until 1871 when it became part of a paint works until demolition.

Excavations in 1977–8 in this location produced much evidence of timber buildings of 13th century and later medieval date.

Anderson of Bourtie's Mansion before demolition

Restored in 1975 by Aberdeen City Council and re-opened as a museum of social and domestic history, this Georgian house – No. 61 Schoolhill – dates from 1769 when it was the most westerly of three houses, originally Nos. 45, 47 and 49 (the last now 61) all similar in design and extending to the corner of Back Wynd. No. 45 is much altered and No. 47 has been replaced by shops and flats (now Nos. 53-59). No. 61 has plain walls of granite, probably Rubislaw, with raised architraves at doors and windows, which have horizontal panes, an early 19th century feature; the back of the house with its projecting stair wing has the original 12-paned windows.

James Dun MA, LLD. (1708-98) was from 1744 the Rector of the Grammar School, then situated on the other side of Schoolhill, and he had this house built – to a design possibly by William Law, Architect – on a site owned by Marischal College. After 1796 the successive owners were Peter Farquharson, Alexander Duff of Echt, John Gordon, and Mary Henderson. After the death in 1884 of Dr William Henderson who lived here from 1838, the property was sold to the School Board, becoming the house of the janitor of the Central School (built 1901).

In 1531 Bishop Gavin Dunbar (1518-31) founded his Hospital for poor Bede-men at the north end of the Chanonry - Map Ref. 93830880. The medieval prebend Manse of Tullynessle lay between it and the Cathedral Kirk. The Hospital was demolished in 1786, in which year it had been handed over to James Forbes of Seaton in exchange for the "Bede House" in Don Street. The Bishop's Hospital for 12 poor men was a building 100ft (30M.) long by 32ft (9.6M.) broad, with roof dormers and a central timber steeple and bell. Inside were 12 small chambers, each with fireplace and chimney; a common kitchen; and an oratory at the east end. Bishop Dunbar died at St. Andrews in March 1531 just after the hospital's founding; it was completed the next year, as was recorded by the following Latin inscription on the south side of the oratory:

> 'Duodecim pauperibus domum hanc Reverendus Pater Gavinus Dunbar hujus almae sedis quondam pontifex aedificari jussit anno a Christo nato 1532
> Gloria Deo'

meaning: 'The reverend father Gavin Dunbar, one-time Bishop of this Cathedral, had this house for 12 poor men built in the year 1532 A.D. Glory be to God'
The south elevation of the hospital had carried panels with the coats-of-arms of King James 5th and the Bishop.

Duncan's Place was a narrow close with, on its south side, No. 1, and also No. 7 High Street; the latter an early 19th century house with walls of coursed granite, two storeys high. Its interesting feature was the piend-roofed gable to the street, and its central dormer window, also piended, at eaves. North of the Place was Nos. 9-11 High Street, also dating from the 1800s, a house with harled walls, of two storeys and attics. These buildings and the close, so typical of the variety of the Aulton vernacular, were demolished in 1971 and replaced by the 2-storey "Elphin-stone House" - No. 7 High Street - very uninteresting in its design and quite lacking the attractive quality of the original good streetscape.

This short street – first mentioned in 1350 – was the medieval "Chack-raw" linking the Castlegate and the Shiprow. It derived its name from the location here of the royal customs house or "Skakkarium", dating from at least the 14th century. Exchequer Court, at No. 9 Exchequer Row, was the probable site, very near the Mint of Aberdeen, which is believed to have stood where once was Stronach's Close and Burnett's Close (No. 5) - Map Ref. 94400628.

One of the Royal Mints of Scotland and reputedly founded by King William the Lyon, it issued coins from Alexander 3rd's reign in the 13th century till the early 16th century. The only remnants of the King's Mint are an oaken panel, removed in 1799 and now at Marischal College, showing the royal arms of James 5th (1513-42) with the initials "V.R" for William Rolland the Master of the Mint; and a much weathered stone tablet also with the Royal Arms, removed from a tenement demolished 1896.

· Royal Arms tablet

Of the later buildings occupying these historic sites, Nos. 1-3 Exchequer Row, demolished 1952, was 18th century in date and three storeys high with coursed granite ashlar frontage; the ground floor had well-proportioned arcaded openings, two windows and two doors, the westmost being the entry pend to Burnett's Close named after Robert Burnett of Elsick whose house, latterly known as Exchequer Place, and dated 1669 with coat-of-arms panel, stood at the end of the Close until removed in 1897. Another demolition (in 1902) was Nos. 60-61 Castle Street - "The Bursar's Hotel", originally the Bursar's House, residence of Dr William Guild, Principal of King's College; born 1586, he died in this house in 1657.

Dating from about 1780, this mansion-No.169 Bon-Accord Street, is two storeys high, with attic having bow dormers; the sunk basement has arched windows. The walls are of harled granite; the base courses, stringcourses and opening surrounds of dressed work. Two bold semi-circular three-window bays flank the main entrance door, with its fanlight and rounded arch, approached by a spacious flight of five steps. The builder was probably George Auldjo of Portlethen - Provost 1791-2 - who owned until 1799 the estate of Clayhills with its pottery and tile factory at Potters' Creek which had been operated by the Auldjo family from about 1750. The Clayhills lands became part of Ferryhill, and from around 1815 this name applied to the house, which has been hotel premises since about 1930.

The original fisher community of Fitty or Futty existed from at least the 13th century as a cluster of houses near where St Clement's Kirk now is, on the north-east shore of the estuary of the Dee. Known in the 14th century as Foty (possibly from the Gaelic "fothach" – marshy land), it is said to have had an early chapel dedicated to St Fotin. The later kirk dating from 1491 was a St Clement dedication. Fitty had been corruptly anglicised to "Footdee" by the early 19th century when it was decided to move the fisher families, because of harbour improvements, to a planned village at the mouth of the Dee. Called "Fish Town" around 1810, it was designed by the city architect John Smith. North and South Squares were laid out during 1808-9 in terraces of one-storey cottages; Middle Row and Pilot Square were added later, and Nos. 1-5 Pier Road, partly two-storey, were also built in the early 1800s. Although different from the usual layout of North-East fishing village rows with their gable-ends to the sea, Fitty is a unique example of a planned group of sturdy granite-built dwellings enclosing their squares and retaining most of the original planning and character, despite some alterations and renewal.

Virginia Street was laid out about 1780 on the Shorelands, a level area reclaimed from the Dee estuary by the building in 1623 of a rough wall - the New Pier - extending from the line of the earlier "Bulwark" or Quayhead dating from 1484.

No. 23 Virginia Street was the Fitty Manse - Map Ref. 94540631 - an attractive mid-18th century house occupied at one time by the minister of St Clement's Kirk. The two-storey granite frontage had sandstone dressed work; excellent classical features included bold eaves mouldings, chimney-copes and a very fine ogee skew moulding at the centre gablet with its keystoned arched window. Internally one room had elaborate plasterwork and a very ornate chimneypiece. The entrance door, flanked by Ionic pilasters with entablature, and dentilled pediment was reached by a flight of shaped granite steps with neat iron handrails. This fine building was approached through a pend with steps up under a piend-roofed harled brick house (Nos. 21-25 Virginia Street), to the west of which was a close and gateway with granite lintel inscribed "1677" and on right of this the initials ◦M◦M ...- other initials to the left were gone.

Manse, pend and gateway were all demolished : 1975.

FITTY PORT

This Port, or gateway, was situated – Map Ref. 94540636 – at the s.e. corner of the Castlegate, and it led by the Fitty-gait to the wee fisher village of Fitty, and the Deemouth; it dated from before 1443 and was still in use as late as 1768. On the broad east gable, partially harled, of the mid-18th century house, No. 4 Castle Terrace, is a recess with two iron hinge-pins, evidently a relic of the old gate. The house, now derelict, was entered by way of a courtyard to the south; there are chamfered window jambs and lintels, and high moulded chimneyheads. The initials "A.C" are inscribed on one skewputt, and another has "I.W" and 1758, the date of the building.

Fitty Quarter was one of the sectors of the town, which in times of defence came under command of a baillie as captain, whose responsibility included the gateway, the fishing community and the Blockhouse at the river-mouth. The city's four "quarters" – Even, Crooked, Green and Fitty – were superseded by municipal wards after 1829.

Nos 4 Castle Terrace and location of Port.

John Forbes of Newe (1741-1821), having made a considerable fortune in Bombay, acquired the estate of Newe which had been sold by his bankrupt cousin Major John Forbes, 9th Laird of Newe. "Bombay Jock's" nephew Charles (1773-1849) succeeded him and became the first baronet of Newe. John Forbes bequeathed £10,000 to the Aberdeen Lunatic Asylum and it is fitting that his monument, this 20M. (65 ft) high red granite obelisk, designed by John Smith in 1830 and originally in St Nicholas Kirkyard, was re-erected in 1838 - under Archibald Simpson's direction - in the grounds of Royal Cornhill Hospital. On three sides of the plinth are inscriptions commemorating the benefactor and his nephew; the fourth gives the dates of the Asylum buildings from the beginning in 1800 till completion in 1855.

The obelisk stands on an apparently natural mound and there is the likelihood, because of its height with a wide view and overlooking the little valley of the Gilcomston burn, that this may be the site of the early motehill or "ton" of Gillecolm who gave his name to the surrounding lands of Gilcomston, and who is mentioned in a Book of Deer charter of about 1130 as Gillecolaim, a contemporary of Ruadri (of Ruthrieston), then Mormaer of Mar.

FOUNTAINHALL CISTERN

Aberdeen's first water supply was from the Loch, but as this became polluted and finally exhausted, by 1706 water began to be brought from Carden's Haugh Well. In 1742 additional supplies were gained from springs and burns west of Gilcomston; six cisterns or fountain-houses were built in 1766 along the old Fountainhall (originally Fountain Haugh) Road – now the east part of Desswood Place. Water was conveyed from these sources to the Water House in Broad Street until 1866. The last of the fountain-houses survived till the late 1880s near where No. 8 Desswood Place – Map Ref. 92520613 – now is, on the north side of the street about 160 yards (145M.) west of Whitehall Road. The little stone-built structure was 7¼ ft. (2.2M.) long by 6½ ft. (2M.) wide with arched stone roof; within the 3½ ft (1.1M.) square interior a bore sunk into the ground collected the rising water and distributed it to supply pipes. In 1903 this wee reservoir was re-built at the Duthie Park – Map Ref. 93780422; above the granite lintel is a bronze tablet with inscription:-

"Old Well from Lands of Fountainhall
Erected in connection with the first City Water Supply
1706."

But the date refers to the earlier Carden Well supply.

Originally built about 1753, probably by Alexander Dyce, merchant, this two-storey mansion has been restored and modernised. The walls are of coursed granite up to the stringcourse above ground floor; from first floor to eaves the stonework is harled. The roof is piend-ended with high chimneys at gables. In 1822 Professor Patrick Copland died here aged 73, his widow occupying the house until 1840. The semi-circular entrance porch dates from around 1830, and the granite gate-piers are surmounted by fine iron urns, late 18th century in date. The name of the house derived from the series of 6 springs, whose fountain-houses formed part of the burgh's water supply after 1766. The house, its grounds much reduced in area, became No. 130 Blenheim Place in 1895.

This beautiful mansion house was built, as dated, in 1773 by Robert Balmanno, whose ancestors were Quakers or Friends, hence the building's name. Balmanno's own name survives in Mannofield, the estate he enclosed, improved and cultivated from the moss-land known as "Foul Moors".

Constructed of good rubble granite the house is two storeys high with attics. Over the central entrance door and its modern coat-of-arms panel is a gablet containing a small semi-circular headed window. The roof is pantiled and the windows are well-proportioned with small panes. On the east wall of a later back addition is a stone lintel inscribed with the date 1812 and the initials J.S. and A.M., referring to the then owners James Shirreffs and his wife Amelia Morrison of Elsick.

Further extensions and restoration work including the garden landscaping were carried out in 1952-3 by Fenton Wyness, the architect, local historian and author. A modern stone tablet in the period garden has the mansion's story inscribed there-on; of note is the wise old Scots motto :-

"Tak Tent O' Time
Ere Time Be Tint"

First mentioned in records in 1350, the Gallowgate was the medieval route to the place of execution, the gallows on Hedonishill beyond the Gallowgate Port. From the end of the 16th century until 1776 the gibbet was on Gallows Hill overlooking the Links, where now the shelter stands at the n.w. corner - Map Ref. 945073 - of Trinity Cemetery.

A large part of the east side of the Gallowgate was cleared in the early 1900s; the only remnants of those 17th and 18th century houses and closes are four inscribed stones built into the dyke at the top of Seamount Stairs. The largest, a "marriage" fireplace lintel, is of red granite inscribed with an anchor and initials D.F. and E.I. The other three were skewputts, one inscribed W.L. and 1764; the second, R.M. and 1679; the third, A.M. and H.F. and dated 1777. One very fine house was that built in 1787 by William Dauney, Architect, for Gilbert Gerard, Advocate, in the close which became Poors Hospital Court (No. 56 Gallowgate) - M.R. 94210663 - when the house was sold as a Girls' Hospital in 1819. It was two-storeyed with steep slated roof and the frontage at the east end of the court was symmetrical with centre pedimented doorway reached by railinged steps. The interior had well-proportioned apartments with good wood panelling and one very fine fireplace flanked by Ionic pilasters. This house was removed in 1905.

On the west side where stood till 1986 the main buildings of the Northern Co-operative Society (Nos. 65-75), dating from 1861 and 1905, there was another handsome 18th century mansion - Dingwall's Court, the town lodging of John Dingwall of Ardo and Rannieston, Provost 1799-1800. A three-storey late 18th century tenement block, Nos. 93-7, north of Henderson's Court, with a plain ashlar granite frontage and splayed window jambs, stood until demolition around 1970, when Nos 99 (J. Beattie's Court), No. 101, No. 103 (Moir's Court) and No. 105 - also 3-storey but simpler in proportion and possibly earlier in date - were also swept away. In 1978 excavations carried out in the pend area of Nos. 45-7 Gallowgate revealed traces of 13th and 14th century timber structures, the pend opening and its original cobbled entry dating from the 15th century.

Gilbert Gerard's House.

GALLOWGATE PORT

Arched House – Nº 173 Gallowgate

This port or fortified gateway was one of six protecting the burgh of Aberdeen in the Middle Ages, and through it passed the old route to the Aulton and to Formartine and Buchan. Also known as the Causey (Causeway) Port, it dated from before 1445; rebuilt in 1518, it was repaired in 1619, and it bore a Royal coat-of-arms panel restored in 1569. To widen the street, its removal was ordered in 1760, but it remained till after 1768. The Port was located near the top of what was Young Street – Map Ref. 941068, this part of Gallowgate being known as Gallowgatehead, and beyond the Port was Causey-End.
Also outwith the gate stood, until demolition with adjoining properties in 1963, No. 173 Gallowgate, for long the oldest remaining house in the street being early 18th century in date. Gable-end to the street, it was built of "heathen" granite boulders with a flat arched pend leading to an inner court and having forestairs giving access from the side lane to the upper floor.

The area of the medieval burgh east of the Gallowgate and Guestrow and north of the Castlegate was known as the Even Quarter; for defence in times of trouble it had one of the baillies as captain.

The stonework of the Firhill Well, or "Gibberie Wallie" - so called, it is surmised, because of gingerbread and other sweeties being sold here by packmen and "gibberie-wifies" - dates from the mid-18th century; the date 1759 is said to have been on the well at one time. According to the bronze inscribed plaque, its chalybeate waters had been noted for their curative properties from at least the year 1721. The well-head and semi-circular stone benching were moved in 1937 from the original site - Map Ref. 937079 - in Firhill Road and re-erected 43 yards (40M.) to the south-west in what is now a park and sports area.

GILCOMSTON CHAPEL OF EASE

On the west side of Summer Street - called Summer Road until around 1770 - the church building, later Gilcomston St Colm's, was built in 1770-1 as a Chapel of Ease, within Oldmachar Parish, for the community of weavers and quarry-working families in the Gilcomston and Loanhead areas. The chapel was built of Loanhead granite, a plain building with few architectural features, the architect-cum-builder being William "Sink 'em" Smith (died 1812), father of the more famous architect John Smith. The Chapel had a notable preacher, Dr James Kidd, who was ordained in 1802. Before his death (1834) Gilcomston had been constituted a parish church; it was renovated in 1878 and extended in 1889.

Renamed Denburn Parish Church after 1976, the building and its famous minister have given near-by streets their names : Chapel Street, where Dr. Kidd had his manse; Kidd Street (Kidd Lane in the 19th century); and Minister's Lane, now re-located, but originally a close between Kidd Street and Skene Street.

A large cairn of stones, possibly a land boundary mark from medieval times, stood where Skene Square and Rosemount Place now meet - Map Ref. 93500674. It had gone before the end of the 18th century but two standing stones, probably the only remains of a prehistoric stone circle dating from about 2000 BC, at the end of the New Stone Age or beginning of the Bronze Age, existed until a century or so ago on the high ground now covered by Hill Street - the approximate site at Map Ref. 93450665. They are recorded on maps between 1746 and 1871, when they stood near the centre of the "Boys' Industrial School" playground. One was 3.6M. (12 ft.), the other about 1.8M. (6ft.) high, and both had gone by 1882 after Hill Street was laid out on the school site.

In early medieval times Gilcomston consisted of a large area to the north-west of the burgh, stretching from the Loch on the east to the Stocket Forest on the west, and bounded by the Denburn valley to the south and by what is now Hilton to the north.

Gilcomston Standing Stones
Conjectural View from south

Greyhope Road links the south side of the Dee mouth with the Bay of Nigg and on the headland stands Girdleness Lighthouse, completed in 1833 and built for the Commissioners of the Northern Lighthouses by the engineer Robert Stevenson, grandfather of the Scots author R.L. Stevenson. The building, circular in plan and tapering to the topmost corb-elled gallery under an iron cupola, is 130ft (39.5M) high; the light is visible up to 19 nautical miles out over the North Sea. From the top the landward view includes many of the Deeside hills, including the Hill of Fare, Clochnaben and Mount Battock, 31 miles (50 Km.) away.

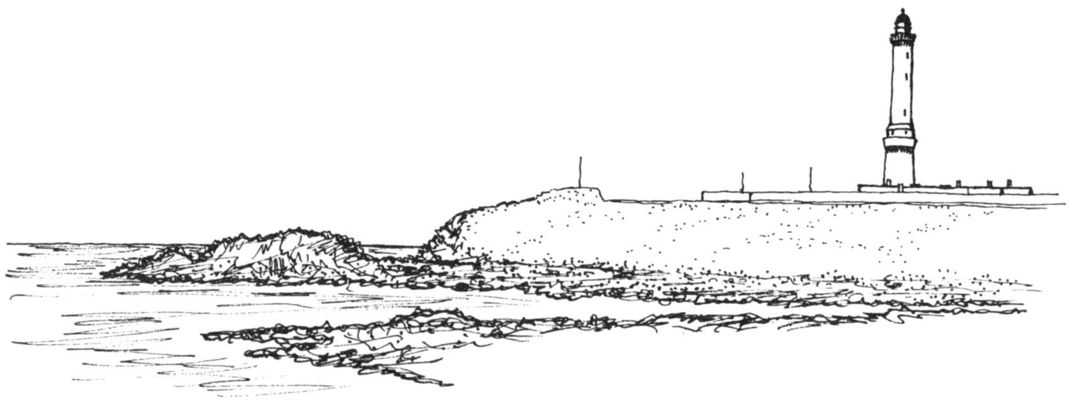

The 16th century Girth Cross, where wrong-doers in the Middle Ages could claim sanctuary from the law, was originally situated in the Bishop's Green - Map Ref. 941087. After the Reformation it became the Mercat Cross of the burgh of Old Aberdeen when it was erected in the middle of the High Street in front of the Town House, until eventually broken up in 1797. Around 1880 the top portion was re-discovered and the cross was restored about 1950. It is a pillar cross on a base of three steps, the shaft being modern; the original top was surmounted by an effigy of the Virgin Mary, and on its four faces there are still the coats-of-arms of the King of Scots, and of the Bishops Elphinstone, Dunbar and William Stewart. It would seem most fitting that, instead of being tucked away in front of the University Geography Department - until 1943 the Old-machar Free Church, later St. Mary's, an Archi-bald Simpson design of 1846 - this unique symbol of the ancient episcopal burgh ought to be returned to its rightful stance in front of the Town House.

Designed in the 1810s, possibly by Archibald Simpson, this fine square of two-storeyed ashlar granite buildings, originally houses, now offices, was completed about 1820 by Simpson and the City Architect, John Smith. The frontages are plain, almost severe Georgian architecture; most of the older six-paned lights have been replaced by less attractive Victorian sash-and-case windows. Cast-iron railings and gates have survived at entrance steps and round the sunk basements. At the North Silver Street side of the low circular wall – once railinged – round the centre of the square stood the well called the Hammermen's Well; the lands on which the square was laid out were the Longlands, belonging to the Hammermen of the Incorporated Trades. The square would be much enhanced if the car parking ceased, with the original garden area reinstated.

No. 3 Golden Square – S.E corner.

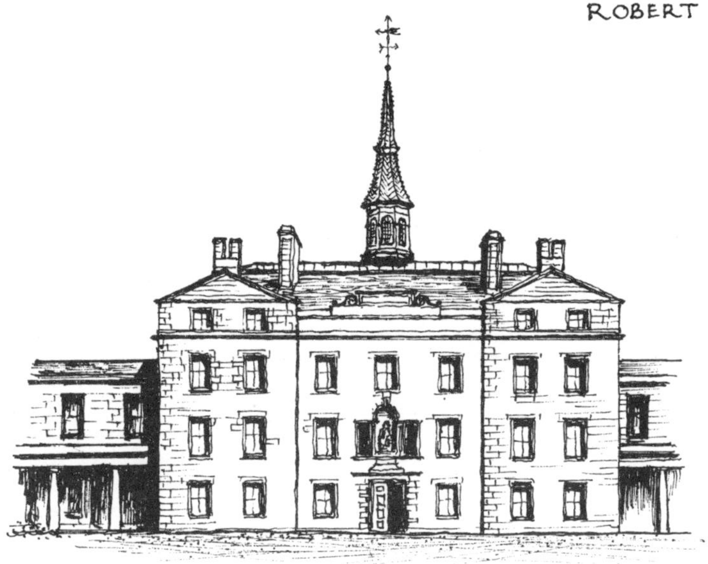

The oldest part, the central block, of the College is the original Hospital for poor boys founded in 1720 by Robert Gordon (1668-1732), a prosperous merchant of Aberdeen and Gdansk, Poland. The architect was William Adam, father of the famed Adam brothers; the Hospital building is four storeys high and built of Loanhead granite with freestone dressed work, the roof surmounted by a graceful central glazed timber spirelet with lead fleche. The straight pediments flanking the recessed centre portion were ogee-shaped originally. Over the moulded doorway in an arched niche is a marble statue of Robert Gordon sculpted by John Cheere of London; the date 1732 is inscribed, building work having started the year before. Completed 1739, the place did not become a boys' boarding school until 1750, as in 1746 it was occupied by the Duke of Cumberland's troops who named it "Fort Cumberland". Although there have been internal alterations, the central stone staircase remains and, at first floor level, the Governors' Room still retains its 18th century quality, elegantly furnished within its fine panelled walls. Projecting from the Hospital block are 2-storeyed wings with colonnades, added in 1830-3 – John Smith, Architect. The back playground entrance gateway with square piers capped by stone balls dates from the mid-18th century; the adjoining high enclosing walls were rebuilt in 1828.

The impressive statue, in the middle of Golden Square, of George, 5th and last Duke of Gordon, dates from 1842. This, the earliest statue in granite and one of the finest, was sculpted by the Aberdeen granite monumental sculptors Macdonald and Leslie, from a model designed by Thomas Campbell, sculptor in London. Removed from its original position in the centre of the Castlegate in 1950, it was re-erected on its present site in 1952; its attraction is considerably marred by the surrounding car park area.

Nos. 1-3 Grant's Place is a pleasant early 18th century corner of the Aulton, a row of picturesque one-storey, granite-built pantile-roofed cottages, with the western gable-end facing on to High Street. An inscribed lintel of one house has the date 1732. The row was restored in 1965, and is now a good example of the local vernacular architecture; as at Wrights and Coopers Place, nearby, the architects were Hurd and Partners, of Edinburgh.

The Green, believed by some historians to be the location of the earliest Aberdeen, a fisherfolk community situated under the pre-Romanesque church on the hill above, is an ancient thoroughfare first recorded in 1273. The name may derive from the Gaelic "grianan" – a sunny spot.

Outwith the town gates, it formed a wide "place" where open-air markets have been held since the Middle Ages. At its west end the south approach to the burgh came across the Denburn, and from its east end narrow streets led to the ports of Netherkirkgate and Shiprow, the latter reached by crossing the Flourmill or Malt Mill Burn at the Malt Mill Brig which was near the top of Exchange Street – Map Ref. 94210612.

The "Green Quarter" of the burgh included the area of the Greengate, the Denburnside and St Katherine's Hill; each quarter in times of unrest came under a baillie/captain for defence.

After Union Street was laid out, the Green ceased as the main route to and from the south; today new developments, existing and proposed, perilously threaten its continued existence, as most of the older properties have already gone.

Dating from before 1750, these two-storeyed houses, Nos. 104-6 High Street, were restored in 1981. They comprise a well-proportioned frontage facing the street with good granite masonry, curved skewputts and moulded chimney copes; above the pend is the name "Greenlaw Court". The gable-end to the street (No. 106) is an interesting feature typical of good Scots burgh street architecture.

Adjoining to the north, No. 108 is earlier; the date 1715 is inscribed on two curved skewputts, that on the n.w. corner has "17" and initials "I.G." - the builder; that at the s.w. has "15" and indechipherable initials, probably of the builder's wife. Beyond this are two old closes, Baillie Place and Market Place, names recalling the former burghal status of Old Aberdeen, and the days when markets were held near the Town House; one market was at Pess (Easter), the other in mid-October.

The Franciscan (Grey) Friary was established in 1469 on land, east of the Broadgate, granted by Richard Vaus of Menie. The old kirk of the Greyfriars was dedicated to the Virgin Mary and stood - Map Ref. 94250646 - just to the south east of Marischal College gateway. The kirk replaced the Franciscans' earlier chapel (c. 1490) and was built by Bishop Gavin Dunbar in 1530; the master-mason was probably Thomas Franche, the whole project being supervised by the churchman Alexander Galloway. It was an aisleless church, measuring internally 118ft (36M.) by 26ft (8M.), and built of Moray sandstone, with massive outer buttresses and steeply pitched roof with small central spirelet. In this building many Aberdonians signed the National Covenant in 1639, and the next year the General Assembly met here.

Instead of restoring and converting the medieval kirk for use as the College Chapel, Aberdeen University had it demolished in 1903, despite widespread protests. The large Gothic east window with its tracery and mullions, and also Bishop Dunbar's much-weathered coat-of-arms above, was incorporated into the present Greyfriars Church - built 1903, A. Marshall Mackenzie, Architect; some of the interior walls have built into them a series of very fine carved timber panels of 17th century date.

The name of this narrow street has, since its first mention in records of 1439, produced much speculation as to whether it derived from "guests" (which originally meant strangers), or from "ghaists" haunting the area from St Nicholas kirkyard, quite some distance to the west.

The Guestrow, between Netherkirkgate at Map Ref. 94300633 and Upperkirkgate at Map Ref. 94170644, was a fashionable residential quarter from the 16th till the 19th century. Here dwelt a cross-section of top Aberdonian society – provosts, bishops, merchants, advocates, lairds, craftsmen, generals and ministers.

On the corner of Blairton Lane stood a typical early 18th century house, No. 57 Broad Street – site M.R. 94220642 – until its demolition with much of Guestrow in 1930. Gable-end facing Broad Street, it was two-storeyed with steep-pitched roofs, rendered walls and granite splay at corner of lane; this was evidently the town lodging of the Milnes of Blairton. The initials of James Milne, who owned Blairton in 1696, are on a heraldic stone, dated 1701 with coat-of-arms and motto, preserved by the city's museum.

Guestrow – looking south from Blairton Lane towards Netherkirkgate.

When most of these properties were swept away around 1930, few discerning eyes could distinguish unique medieval townscape from relatively modern accretions and slum squalor. Like Broad Street and Shiprow, and much of the two Kirkgates the Guestrow has become only a memory of what was once an historic and thriving neighbourhood in the heart of our city.

HARDGATE WELL

The old south road – the Hardgate – from the burgh's west outskirts to the crossing of the Dee, can still be followed; as a main route it was superseded by Holburn Street, begun in 1807 and completed 1811.

The Hardgate Well in its arched recess, about 3ft (900mm) high, in the east wall of what was Strawberry Bank gardens – Map Ref. 93520577 – was opened up and rebuilt in 1970, as dated on the bronze information tablet; the well had been blocked up about 1840. It is said that at the 2nd Battle of Aberdeen (or the Battle of the Justice Mills) in 1644 this well was filled with the blood of the casualties.

Hardgate Well and Strawberry Bank in 1950

The entry gateway with steps between square granite pillars, linked by a wrought-iron arch and empty lamp bracket is the only sad remnant of Strawberry Bank and its once-pleasant cottages with south-facing gardens. This row of little houses, one with centre pediment and conservatory-type dormer, were built around 1830 and demolished about 1969.

Hardweird is now but a name and a memory of an old street situated – Map Ref. 93510637 – between Jack's Brae and the Skene Street steps, running almost parallel to Upper Denburn. The name derived from a croft of the same name, and possibly refers to a strongly-fenced enclosure: "Hard" meaning strong, and "Weird" (Scots) meaning ward. Before being cleared away as slums by 1938, the buildings, 18th century in date and originally occupied mostly by Gilcomston mill-workers and their families, were single and two storey red-tiled cottages, several with forestairs to upper floors. Before the days of its deterioration, Hardweird displayed the informal and picturesque layout typical of the small-scale street architecture of an old Scottish burgh.

Hardweird – looking towards Skene Row with street well at corner of Upper Denburn

The lands of Hislehead were originally part of the Freedom lands, and of the ancient Forest of Stocket granted by King Robert 1st to the burgh in 1319. But many portions were feued off in 1551, when Hazlehead was feued to Robert Chalmers, later passing to other families including the Mortimers in the late 17th century. Around 1775 William Rose acquired the lands and built the mansion house - MapRef. 89280537 - where he lived till 1834; the Roses were prosperous ship-owners. The main house was of simple but dignified proportions, of two storeys and attic, with curved skewputts and wide chimney gables; later additions were the entrance porch, with its classical details, dating from the 1820s, and the back wing, including a circular stair tower with pointed roof. In 1920 the City Corporation acquired house and estate from the Rose family. The grounds became public parkland and golf courses, but by 1958 the old mansion was taken down to be replaced by a restaurant building of uninspired design.

The walled garden, now very overgrown, still exists - MapRef. 88850543; although the stone walls are ruinous, the east gate opening retains its granite lintel inscribed in fine Roman lettering "W.F.R.1831.H.F.R." referring to William Rose and his wife. At the park entrance is the gate-lodge, one-storey and Tudor in style, with a central porch and timber columned veranda, dating from about 1826 - John Smith, Architect.

Only the site remains of this building - Map Ref. 93660808 - also known as the House on the Hill; even the Firhill it stood on has been levelled. The Hermitage, located in what was part of the grounds of Powis House, was erected probably by Hugh Leslie of Powis in 1781; it was a three-storey brick building with an underground basement and a flat roof with railing. About 1830 the roof was altered to a round pointed shape and thatched. This interesting wee structure was demolished in 1925 and its remains were removed in 1927 when the hill became a sandpit. The levelled area, between Meston Walk (originally College Wynd) and Hermitage Avenue, is enclosed by fencing and occupied by a collection of ugly huts.

HIGH SCHOOL FOR GIRLS

The central building of this school in Albyn Place – now co-educational and called Harlaw Academy – was designed by Archibald Simpson, Architect, and built 1837-9 as Mrs Emslie's Institution, or Female Orphan Asylum, which became after 1892 the Girls' High School.
The fine but austere classical frontage of two storeys has a high arched doorway flanked by four pilasters, and there are pedimented side wings. The original design was considerably altered when the two adjoining houses, dating from about 1830, were incorporated in the enlarged school. Both these villas were two-storeyed, No. 19 Albyn Place having a porch with Grecian Doric fluted columns, the porch of the house to the west having Roman Doric columns.

From College Bounds to the Town House this was the main street of the Aulton and many of its old and picturesque buildings have survived from the mid-18th century.

On the west side Brewery Lane is flanked on the south by Nos. 17-19 High Street, a two-storeyed harled house of around 1800 with raised architraves at door and windows. North of the Lane, No. 21, built about 1750, has a chimney gable to the street, curved skew-putts, pantiled roof and chamfered jambs and lintels. Nos. 41 and 43 are also cottages of the old style with gables to the street. Nos. 57-61 is two-storey with central gablet at wallhead; one skewputt is dated 1821 with initials "I.C.B." No. 81 is an interesting Georgian mansion of around 1780, set back in its garden with granite pillared gateway to the street; a two-storey harled house, the centre pediment has a round-arched window at first floor and the doorway has a rectangular fanlight.

Nº 70 High Street

On the east side of the street, opposite Thom's Place - a little row of houses with pantiled roofs - there stands an excellent classical mansion at No. 70 dating from about 1820; a two-storey building with dentilled cornice under eaves, the central columned doorway being flanked by curved three-window bow projections. No. 90 is early 19th century, with gable-end to the street, rubble walls and pantiled roof.

HILTON STONE

Scheduled as an Ancient Monument, this monolith, known also as the "Lang Steen", stands in the playground of Hilton Academy - Map Ref. 92230836. It is a 10ft. (3M.) high granite stone and may have originated as part of a now-disappeared Bronze Age stone circle of about 1500 BC. The stone's original location was to the east of its present position which is approximately the site of Hilton House, also known as Caprastoun, built in 1729 by Dr. James Gordon of the Pitlurg family; it was demolished in 1925 when the estate became a housing development.

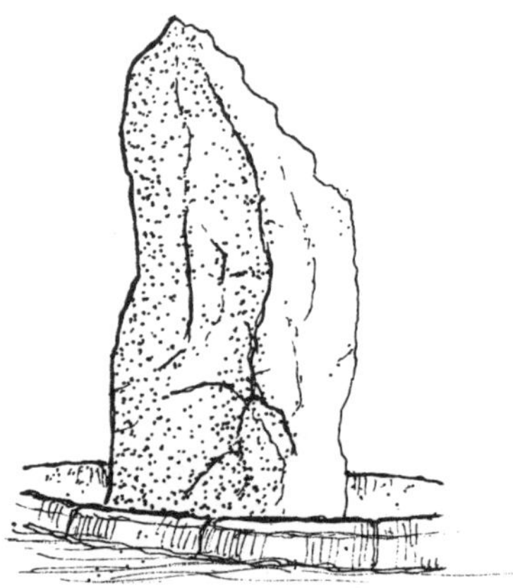

A small house with an attractive name, this was an 18th century two-storeyed building with a red pantiled roof; it stood some two hundred yards - 180M - west of Morningfield Hospital midway between what are now King's Gate and Morningfield Road - Map Ref. 91540612. Typical of other countryside dwellings round the outskirts of Aberdeen, it survived demolition till around 1933. Its particular interest is that here the young George Gordon aged 10-11 years spent holidays in 1798, the year he left the town of his boyhood, never to return; after a brief lifetime of literary acclaim as Lord Byron the poet, he died in Greece in 1824.

Broad Street and Huxter Row around 1850

Huxter Row - huckster means a small trader or pedlar - was a short street, also known as Booth Raw, at the west end of the Castlegate; it was removed in 1867 when the Town House at the corner of Broad Street was built. The tavern "The Lemon Tree" - No. 7 Huxter Row, and the house where Robert Gordon of Gordon's College was born in 1655 were also cleared away then. Today the site of the Row is more or less occupied by Concert Court, where Advocates Hall was built in 1869. At the corner of Broadgate and Huxter Row (Map Ref. 94330634) there stood a very good example of a 17th century town lodging, four storeys high with a splendid round angle turret capped by a conical roof.

Scotland's first portrait painter, one of an artistic family, was George Jamesone, born in 1588 in one of the burgh's finest town-lodgings situated on the north side of Schoolhill and opposite St Nicholas kirkyard. Demolished in 1886, its site – Map Ref. 94050635 – is marked by an inscribed bronze plaque on the wall of Nos. 22-26 Schoolhill. Jamesone, after attending the Grammar School and Marischal College, studied in Flanders and Italy. After being appointed King's Limner by Charles 1st, whose portrait he painted, he worked in Edinburgh, returning to live in his Schoolhill house from about 1625 until his death in 1644. The building had a forecourt and a front projecting wing which had, at both corners at first floor, corbelled round turrets, whose conical roofs were removed about 1850. A stair turret was corbelled out between first and second floors in the angle of the main house and the front wing; the arched entrance door had above it the Latin inscription "Domus Optima Caelo." On the east gable was a pend leading to Donald's Court. This handsome T-plan lodging, similar in style to its contemporaries Ross's House, Mar's Castle and old Trinity Hall was built in 1586 – the work of the master-mason Andrew Jamesone, father of the painter.

Lower Justice Mills

Known originally as the Justiciar's Mills and first mentioned in 1349, these consisted of the Upper Mill, situated south of the junction of Holburn Street and Justice Mill Lane – Map Ref. 93320568; and the Lower Mill – Map Ref. 93370562 – in Union Glen. The battle of 1644 was fought nearby on the brae above the den of the Howe Burn, later mis-named into the anglicisation: Hol-burn. Nothing remains today of the corn mills; the Upper Mill, an L-plan building, was demolished when the Regent, now Odeon, Cinema was built in 1932, the Lower Mill, a T-shaped building surviving till the 1960s. The former's water supply was from a dam sited south of the corner of Alford Lane and Holburn Street, the dam being fed from the West Burn of Rubislaw by a lade which followed the line of what is now Union Lane. The Lower Mill dam was halfway down the east side of the steep brae above the mill.

Built into a wall on the east side of Alford Lane about 10yards (9M.) from Holburn Street is one of the Inner March Stones marked C.R. (City Royalty); in its original location it had been the "Doupin' Steen" where newly-elected burgesses were ritually and painfully initiated.

One of the two east gateways of the burgh was the Justice or Thieves' Port, the last of the ports to be erected. Built in 1440 it spanned Justice Street where it at one time narrowed near the end of Justice Lane – Map Ref. 94550642. Sometimes known colloquially as "the Port", Justice Street was earlier called Justice Wynd, perhaps originally and more accurately Justiciar's Wynd. It led to the place of execution which in the early Middle Ages was the Heading Hill, and later it was the passage to the Gallow Hill reached by way of the Park Road over Thieves' Brig – Map Ref. 94650685 – which crossed a wee burn long since channelled underground. The last execution on Gallow Hill was in 1776. The Justice Port was cleared away in 1789 and the street was widened and improved after 1883 when many old buildings were removed, including several narrow lanes and closes such as the Cowgate, Pensioner's Court, Mauchlin Tower Court, Bothwell Court and Masson's Court.

At the north end of Justice Street, approximately where the traffic roundabout is now, was the Angel Well – Map Ref. 947 065 – dating from about 1558, and now built over, but at one time enclosed by a wall. Nearby Wales Street, swept away by 1959 when Beach Boulevard was laid out, was known as Well Street in the early 19th century.

Justice Street about 1850

The lands of Kepplestone - the old spelling was Caplestone - are now divided by Viewfield Road, on the west side of which is St Lukes, originally known as Kepplestone Cottage, a single-storey harled building dating from around 1800. It belonged to Thomas Curr, tea merchant in Schoolhill, around 1876; it was acquired thereafter by the notable artist Sir George Reid RSA. who changed the name to St Lukes and built a two-storey extension with oriel windows - William Kelly, Architect. The rear studio of about 1900 is of harled granite with high large windows and a picturesque round tower with conical slated roof. Since 1961 the building has been the Regimental Museum of the Gordon Highlanders and also the Regimental H.Q. The Gordon Highlanders have been the local regiment of Aberdeen and the North-East since it was raised in 1754. West of St. Lukes is a two-storey stable block with an outside stair to first floor, and beyond a gate is the old walled garden sloping to the Hazlehead or West Rubislaw Burn which becomes the now-underground Howe or Holburn nearer the city centre.

William Elphinstone, Bishop of Aberdeen (1483-1514) founded King's College in 1494 when he obtained from Pope Alexander 6th a papal "bulla" authorising the establishment of a University in Old Aberdeen. First dedicated to the Virgin Mary, the College became known as King's, James 4th being its patron. Building work began in 1500; the Chapel, dated 1504, with its famous Crown steeple, is an excellent example of the late Scottish Gothic style, and was complete by 1506. An impressive landmark in the Aulton, it is the finest architecture in the city. From the early 17th century the building was used for graduations and synod meetings and not as a chapel; the west end was the library from 1773, after Bishop Stewart's library-built against the south wall-was burnt, until 1870. The interior has the original wooden stalls and screens, probably by John Fendour and the best surviving pre-Reformation examples in all Scotland; seven windows have excellent stained glass designed by Douglas Strachan between 1903-1938. The Crown fell in a storm in 1633 and was rebuilt by master-mason George Thomson, under the direction of Dr William Gordon, Professor of Medicine. Outside the west door is the large bronze and marble monument to the founder Bishop Elphinstone, with its interesting eulogistic inscriptions in 16th century Gaelic; originally inside the Chapel, the tomb was reconstructed in 1926 by the artist Henry Wilson.

The sturdy building at the north-east corner of the College quadrangle was known as the New Work or the Square Work when built in 1657, the year General Monk arrived in Aberdeen as Cromwell's local commander. He deposed William Guild as Principal and appointed John Row. Rectangular in plan, Cromwell Tower, as it came to be called in the mid-19th century, was built as residential quarters – walls of rubble stonework, six storeys high with chambers for 24 students. To build it contributions came from the masters and others, including Cromwellian officers in the area. In 1825, when the residence of students within the college was no longer compulsory, the block was converted into three floors of classrooms: John Smith, Architect. The flat roof is surrounded by a corbelled parapet, and the original design of the tower may have been influenced by the architectural tradition of the North-east towerhouse castles.

Bishop Gavin Dunbar built, around 1525, the original College courtyard which, with a cloister-type arcade on the south side, was of smaller area than the present quadrangle; there were two round towers at the south-east and south-west corners. The old well of 1505 was rediscovered and restored in 1937; of the circular towers, that at the s-e, known as the Dunbar or Ivy Tower (1525) remains, somewhat altered. It is approximately 20ft. (6M.) in diameter, with walls about 3¼ft. (1M.) thick. The original wooden spirelet was blown down in 1715; the roof is now conical and slated. The rubble-built tower, four storeys high, is now partly enclosed by the library which in 1892 replaced the Old Hall. The south side of the quad also dates from 1892, while the west frontage and entrance gateway are in Tudor Gothic style (1825-6) by John Smith, Architect.

No. 142 King Street

The south end of this street was laid out in 1801-3 by David Hamilton, the Glasgow architect, as the first part of the route from the Castlegate to the Bridge of Don. Apart from Archibald Simpson's Episcopal Cathedral, Medico-Chirugical Hall and Nos 1-5 (1839); and Nos. 7-9 by Gillespie Graham, Architect in 1836, the street was mostly planned by John Smith (1781-1852), appointed in 1824 as City Architect and Superintendent of Public Works. An attractive feature of the streetscape is the arcading of ground floor doors and windows as at Nos. 11-23 (about 1835) on the west side. No. 27 is a Neo-Greek building designed by Smith in 1833 as the County Record Office, now Customs and Excise. The impressive corner at Nos. 67-107 and 2-7 West North Street (1827) was demolished in 1983 and rebuilt nearby; other Smith designs are Nos. 133-141 (1828) and the blocks Nos. 143-5 and 159-173 (late 1830s), No. 159 having a fine arched pend.

On the east side is the prominent four-storey corner tenement at Nos. 2-10 King Street and 1-8 Castle Street by John Smith (1822); Nos. 12-18 dates from about 1825, and of the same date is another grand curved three-storey block - Nos. 50-56 King Street, at the corner of East North Street.

The earliest part of King Street, built before 1809, is Nos. 82-144, including No. 142, in a back court reached through a pend; this was built by John Smith as his own residence and architectural office. The entrance doorway is surmounted by a Latin motto - "Humani Nihil Alienum" - (All humanity is my concern), and the porch has stuccoed Greek Doric columns. The pedimented west frontage is harled with dressed stonework at openings; the plinth is granite. The building is now used as club premises.

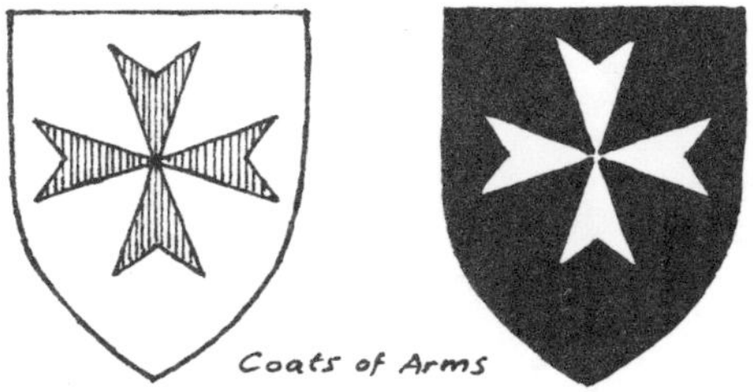

Coats of Arms

Knights Templars Knights Hospitallers

In 1957 a bronze tablet was set in the wall on the west side of Justice Lane, now the market stance, to mark the site of the house or "tenement" of the Templars where now stands the R.C. Chapel of St Peter in Chapel Court – Map Ref. 94520647. The Knights Templars held property in Aberdeen in the early 13th century, but after the abolition of their Order in 1312, their tenement passed to the Knights of the Hospital of St. John of Jerusalem till the Reformation of 1560. The building north of the Justice Port was quite ruinous by the mid-17th century. More than 100 years later, the Catholics acquired the site, and between 1803 and 1817 they built the small St. Peter's Chapel – James Massie, Architect – in an attractive style of Regency "Gothick"; Chapel Court is approached through an arched pend with gateway and recessed piers. This chapel was the main R.C. church in Aberdeen until 1860, when the Cathedral of St. Mary of the Assumption (Alexander Ellis, Architect) was built in Huntly Street.

LANG STANE

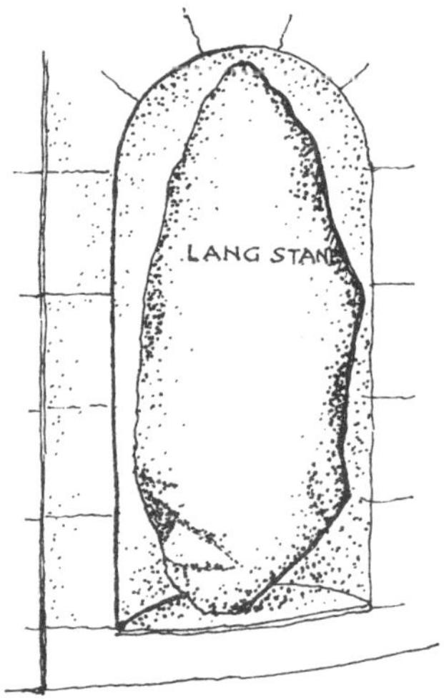

This is a roughly dressed slab of grey granite - just under 6ft. (1.75M.) high and 2 ft. (600mm.) wide - set upright in a niche at the north-west corner of Dee Street and Langstane place. The stone was inscribed "Lang Stane" probably about 1850, but it had stood near its present location before the mid-18th century. It was possibly either a march stone or part of a now-vanished stone circle. If the latter, the Crab Stane, situated some 300 yards (275M.) to the south-west, was perhaps part of the same prehistoric monument.

Also known as the "Bede House", Nos. 20-22 Don Street is a very good 17th century house of the old Scots domestic style; T-shaped in plan. The house, restored in 1965, has slated roofs and was originally harled. The street windows are surrounded by roll-mouldings as is the archway of Hay's Pend which leads under the house to the entrance below the corbelled turret of the piend-roofed staircase wing. Above the door is a stone panel with a Latin inscription and the date 1676 - the year in which Baillie William Logan built the house; he was a Baillie in 1661. The property belonged to Sir Thomas Gordon of Cluny about 1615 when he renounced it in favour of Alexander Lillie, whose heirs sold to Logan. The house belonged to James Forbes of Seaton before 1786, when he exchanged it for Bishop Dunbar's Hospital for 12 poor men, which he then had demolished. But Logan's Lodging became the Bede House for only two decades or so, for by 1800 the Bede-men ceased to occupy it, receiving instead a monthly grant, as they still do today. The Lodging is now converted into flats.

The fine mansion, Nos. 4-5 Mackie Place dates from after 1760 and is remarkable for its twin front gables, the ogee curves of which have similarities to those of the demolished Raeden House and of the original gables of Gordon's Hospital. The house - one of Aberdeen's early buildings of quarried granite - is semi-detached, the two doors being central and approached by attractive curved flights of steps. Mackie Place takes its name from Robert Mackie, skinner, who was feuing the ground along the Denburnside here in the latter half of the 18th century. At that time Nos 4-5, reached by the wee bridge across the burn, would have had a picturesque situation, but today it is quite dominated by surrounding tenement blocks.

Just west of Mackie Place was the "Galleries", almost opposite the end of Whitehouse Street. Here, until its demolition in the 1920s, stood the White House. This was a gaunt five-storey high building with one well-fenestrated elevation having pilasters at the corners. Its lofty brick gable was ogee-shaped with a central round-headed window, this feature indicating a dating contemporary with Nos. 4-5.

This well-house - a Scheduled Ancient Monument - stood originally near the middle of the Castlegate. Known as the "Mannie Well" because of the charming lead statuette on top, with four grotesque metal masks at the corners, it was set up (1708) by William Lindsay, goldsmith and water overseer. The well has the date 1755, when it was moved to the east end of the Castlegate where it more or less occupied the site of the Laigh or Fish Cross (a simple upright stone shaft on a raised platform), which was cleared away in 1742: the fish market being then moved to the foot of Shore Brae. In 1840 the well-house was taken down to be re-erected 12 years later in the Green on the site of an older well there. A picturesque and familiar landmark, it overlooked the Green's popular Friday markets for over a century. Dismantled in 1958, it was once more rebuilt in 1972 at the west end of the Castlegate as a feature of the re-established Plainstanes. This paved area, two steps high and 84ft (25M) long by 57ft (17M) wide, had extended west of the Mercat Cross from about 1752, but had been removed in 1842 when the Cross was re-sited further east to its present location.

Dignified by the name of "castle" this toun-lodging in the Gallowgate was dated 1595 as inscribed on a skewputt on the front gable; two other skewputts had carved on them the letters "T.R.", evidently the initials of the builder. The "castle" is believed to have been the town-house of the Earls of Mar during the 17th century; it stood within the Gallowgate Port on the east side of the street—Map Ref. 94120674. It was an L-shaped building, with one wing projecting, the top storey above a double corbel course, and a coat-of-arms panel halfway up the wall-face. The roof was pantiled and in the angle of the wing a small round stair turret was corbelled out. The similarity between Mar's Castle and Provost Ross's House (1593) is remarkable, and another vanished building, old Tarnty Ha' (Trinity Hall) was also similar in design; these three buildings were contemporary in date and possibly the work of the same master-mason Andrew Jamesone, father of George Jamesone the painter. In 1836 Mar's Castle was repaired and lost much of its character. Like Ross's House it had a small forecourt, which was at this time removed; the lower floor was altered and the fine corbelling details covered by harling. As with many of Aberdeen's old "lodgings" there were two tenements, one "foreland" and one "inland". Under the south gable was a pend called Reid's Court, a close leading to a garden with summer-house. Mar's Castle—an excellent example of a medieval town-house—was swept away during street improvements in the Gallowgate in 1897.

This lane was so-called because it was on the line of the Inner March of the burgh and a march stone marked "C.R." for City Royality still stands at its east end; the lane itself was swept away when the Jack's Brae properties were demolished around 1939. The Brae, first mentioned in 1758 was named after John Jack, a neighbouring proprietor. Some of its houses were occupied by millworkers in the nearby Gilcomston Mill - known as Strachan's in the 19th century - in Leadside Road; the mill existed from before 1773 and its buildings were demolished in 1984. An even older mill, also driven by the Leadside Road lade, stood at Gilcomston Brae (now the east part of Baker Street); here a corn mill had existed since around 1400.

At the west end of March Lane is No. 3 Mackie Place -- a much-altered house known as Murlingden in the 19th century; the oldest part with the symmetrical three-light windows and one ogival gable-end is similar to other nearby houses. It dates from 1776 after the area was feued out by Robert Mackie about the year 1760.

Nº 3 Mackie Place

MARINE TERRACE

Marine Terrace, originally to be called Belvidere Terrace, was designed by Archibald Simpson, Architect, in 1831. Building began in 1837 but only two houses were completed then; the rest of the terrace on the west side of this one-sided street was not finished until about 1877. The central two houses (Nos. 7-8) are two-storeyed with basements, and are flanked by longer terraces of single-storey houses Nos. 3-6, and 9-11, all having attractive entrance doors approached by steps with railings. Although the original design was not carried out as Simpson intended with two-storey blocks at the north and south ends, this quiet and dignified terrace, its frontage linked by a continuous bold cornice, preserves the essential graciousness of Georgian architecture; this, despite the execrable excrescences added in 1967 at each end.

Mariscchal College in the 18th century.

Marischal College In Broad Street was founded by George Keith 5th Earl Marischal in 1593; he intended it as a separate and "rival" University to Kings College. It was originally housed within the old conventual buildings of the Greyfriars whose 16th century church became the College Kirk. The entrance - College Gate - was through a pend from the Broadgate; the narrow arched gateway built about 1623 had above it the Keith coat-of-arms. The college buildings, including a 7-storey high tower on the north-west, were extended in 1676 and 1694; the south wing, plain and piend-roofed, was built in 1747 by the architect William Adam. These tenement-like buildings incorporated parts of the old friary; the Principal's Chamber had a fine wood-panelled ceiling with 18 coats-of-arms of former principals and college benefactors. This old college was replaced, between 1836 and 1844 by a new building, in an austere style of Tudor Gothic, round three sides of a quadrangle, the architect being Archibald Simpson. As it stands today the college was completed after the Greyfriars Kirk, following bitter controversy, was demolished, and the granite frontage on to Broad Street, with the other extensions, including the great Mitchell Tower and Hall were erected in 1893-1906. Marischal and Kings had merged in 1860 to become the University of Aberdeen.

This was the toun lodging of the Keiths, Earls Marischal and it stood midway along the south side of the Castlegate – Map Ref. 94450632; its site is now the top of Marischal Street. It was demolished in 1767 to make way for the completion the next year of the new street down to the harbour. The Hall dated from about 1540, for it was evidently the Abbot of Deer's town house before becoming Keith property at the Reformation. Built round a quadrangular courtyard with high conical-roofed corner towers, it had been the most imposing mansion in Aberdeen in the Middle Ages, and was occupied by Queen Mary in 1562 after her victory at Corrichie; from a window she is said to have witnessed the beheading, on the steps of the Tolbooth opposite, of Sir John Gordon, captured at the battle. In the courtyard the Covenanting Commissioners from Edinburgh preached in 1638, the town's kirks being closed to them. When the house was removed, the ornate 17th century sundial from the Earl Marischal's garden, which stretched down as far as the harbour, was later set up in the garden of Rubislaw House until its demolition in 1886; it is now at the House of Schivas.

Earl Marischal's sundial.

Now a hotel, this two-storey building, Nos. 13-15 Market Street, with its interesting classical style frontage, was built in 1845 by Archibald Simpson, the architect who laid out Market Street in 1840. The Institute's classrooms and hall provided for training and instruction of trades apprentices and craftsmen and its library contained 16,000 books; it was the forerunner of Gray's Art School, Aberdeen School of Architecture and Robert Gordon's Institute of Technology.

The building's street facade has a central doorway surmounted by a three-light window feature with Roman Doric columns under the pediment. The ground floor openings were all originally arcaded, but the upstreet windows have been spoiled by later alterations, including plate-glazing and signboard fascias.

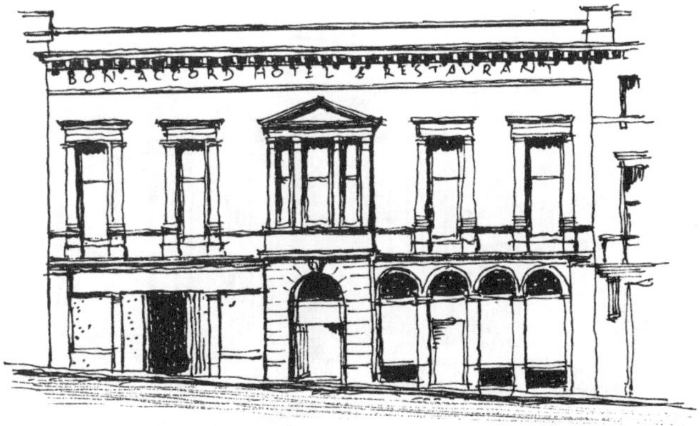

Built in 1818-20, this Archibald Simpson building -No.29 King Street- is a very attractive design in the Classical style with an entrance portico of four Greek Ionic columns and entablature and pediment. This frontage is a foretaste of the same architect's similar but grander facade for the Assembly Rooms in Union Street. Now part of the Customs and Excise Offices, No.29 was erected for the Aberdeen Medico-Chirurgical Society - founded 1789 - who no longer use it as their library and meeting hall. The flanking building to the south, No.27, designed originally as the Record Office by John Smith, Architect, is also now a government-owned office building.

The extension to the north, No.31, also by John Smith, completes the balanced symmetry of this excellent street frontage in the classical Grecian style.

In the Castlegate stands the Mercat Cross - a Scheduled Ancient Monument - regarded as the finest burghal cross in Scotland. It was built in 1686 by John Montgomery, Master-mason of Old Rayne, and originally stood, in front of the Tolbooth, on the site of an earlier High Cross, also called the "flesche croce". On its west side was the Plainstanes, a raised paved area set out in 1752. In 1821 the Cross was repaired - John Smith, Architect, and for some years after 1822 its arcades were built up when it became the town's post-office; in 1842 it was moved to its present position.

The Cross is hexagonal in plan, having six arches under an entablature decorated with medallions comprising bas-relief carvings of the heads of ten Stewart monarchs: James 1st to James 5th, Mary, James 6th, Charles 1st and 2nd, and James 7th. Save for the granite base and steps, the structure is of sandstone, including the shaft, with its elaborately carved floral design, surmounted by a sculptured unicorn and shield displaying the arms of the King of Scots.

The most notable of Aberdeen's fairs, the "Timmer" Market - where wooden vessels and implements were sold - was held in the Castlegate on the last Wednesday of August; changed to the fourth Thursday of that month, but since 1935 it has been held in nearby Justice Lane.

This old house stood on the south side of Great Northern Road - Map Ref. 915096; it was the mansion house of the estate of Lower Middlefield which formed part of the lands of Old Cruives (Woodside). William Mosman who bought the lands in 1754 from his brother Thomas, was a limner (painter) in Aberdeen and taught drawing, architecture and perspective at both University Colleges. He built this house just before 1770 when the lands were advertised for sale, including the "excellent new house" and a garden, with a high thick dyke, to the west of and behind the house. The two-storey granite mansion was a plain symmetrical building and above the centre doorway was a broad gablet at roof level with a semi-circular headed window with arched stringcourse over, surmounted by a chimney-head. Demolished in 1954, the site of the house is now occupied by flats.

Migvie House - No. 23 North Silver Street - has been government offices since 1914. The house, approached through square granite gate-pillars is of pleasing proportions. The ashlar granite facade has a recessed central portion containing the entrance door with flight of steps retaining the original railings; the base courses are of rustic granite masonry at basement level. The gables have small arched windows under broad chimneys, heightened by later brickwork. Migvie House was built in 1839 for Dr. MacRobin, Professor of Medicine at Marischal College, and occupied by him till 1879. Later it became for a period the West St. Nicholas Manse. Despite some alterations the interior still displays good plasterwork ceilings and fine panelled doors; the stairway has stone treads, with a cast-iron baluster and mahogany handrail.

MITCHELL'S HOSPITAL

In its secluded and pleasant setting this Hospital – No. 9 Chanonry – was founded, as dated, in 1801 by David Mitchell for the maintenance of five widows and five unmarried daughters of burgesses. The building, surrounded by its garden and trees, forms three sides of a wee court with a sundial in the middle. The one-storey accommodation was originally dining-hall, kitchen and bedrooms. The gable ends of the wings are piended and there is a small bell-cote placed centrally, below which is an inscribed tablet commemorating the founder. A single storey extension at the south-west was added at a later date, and the Hospital was converted in 1924 into four self-contained cottages, and further modernised in 1965. It occupies the site of the pre-Reformation prebend manse of Banchory-Devenick.

There are records of an earlier hospital in the Aulton built 1711 by the Trade Guilds, but discontinued in 1792.

Belmont Street was laid out in 1784 and later joined to Union Street in 1803, but this house, No. 37, preceded the street; it was built during the 1770s as a town-house by George Moir, 6th laird of Scotstown, an "improving" landlord. As proprietor of the Spital area he carried out improvements to his lands near the Links around 1780. In 1752 George Moir had succeeded his father Alexander Moir, the 5th laird, who was a prominent Jacobite in the 1715 Rising and went into exile in the Netherlands. The Belmont Street house is two-storeyed with basement, and was altered in 1848 and 1901. Its fine frontage with a bold cornice and doorway flanked by the original double stairs had its handsome appearance ruined by the alterations of 1927 involving a projecting shopfront quite out of keeping with the Georgian design. Internally some good plasterwork and woodwork survived.

George Moir died in 1789, and was succeeded by his son Alexander who sold the house in 1806 to John Menzies of Pitfodels who died, the last of his family, in 1843. The panel carved with the Royal and Menzies coats-of-arms which was brought here by John Menzies in 1806, after the demolition of Pitfodels Lodging in the Castlegate, was built into a back wall behind No. 37, but in 1983 it was set up in Collison's Aisle, St. Nicholas Kirk.

Nº 37 Belmont Street · around 1850.

The Netherkirkgate, first mentioned 1382, was the lower road to the Town Kirk until blocked up by a shopping development in 1964. The Port or gate dated from before 1443 and was eventually removed about the year 1770. Its location – Map Ref. 94210629 – was approximately at the south end of the former narrow Flourmill Lane and near where McCombie's Court joins the Netherkirkgate on the east side. In the Middle Ages the defence of the gateway was the charge of the Captain-Baillie of the "Crooked" Quarter of the burgh in times of war or unrest – the quarter extended northwards from the Shiprow, and to the west of the Guestrow and the Gallowgate.

Before its demolition (1964), Nos. 54-56 Netherkirkgate was an early 18th century building, three storeys high with granite walls and chamfered surrounds to upper windows. Skewputts at eaves were finely moulded, that to the east over the corner of Flourmill Lane being of granite, while the west one, of red sandstone, had carved on it the initials I·MC and the date of building 1727. In the 19th century the ground floor was much altered as a shop, the upper window glazing was changed and dormers added to the roof.

Nos 54-6 Netherkirkgate before demolition.

The New Inn in the Castlegate - for long the main hostelry in the town - was a plain, solid three-storey building standing where the Clydesdale Bank is today. Built in 1755 this inn lodged many famous travellers and visitors to Aberdeen during the latter half of the 18th and early 19th century. Above the hostelry on the third floor was the Freemasons' Lodge, hence Lodge Walk, the name of the pend and close east of the Tolbooth. Both the New Inn and the Lodge were cleared away in 1839 when the present building, to Archibald Simpson's design, was built for the North Bank, founded 1836. Regarded as a Simpson masterpiece, despite the heaviness of the top cornice and balustrade which accentuate the insignificant base, it has a grand corner portico, with lofty Corinthian columns, surmounted by a terra-cotta sculptured group by James Giles (1801-1870) - artist colleague of Simpson. The interior is notable for the impressive banking hall with Corinthian pilasters and a gilded Parthenon frieze.

The New Inn about 1800

Dating from 1842, after Market Street was laid out, this Archibald Simpson building, at the corner of Hadden Street, was destroyed by fire in 1882 and rebuilt thereafter. Of the original design the very impressive Market Street entrance facade, bold and simple granite massing in a style reminiscent of the early Egyptian temples, was a masterpiece in the handling of the local building stone. The interior consisted of an arcaded round-ended market hall approximately 320ft (98M.) long with shops in aisles at first floor level. After its regrettable demolition in 1971 it was replaced by the present shopping centre building which is far inferior to, and lacks the striking quality of, the Simpson design.

In adjacent Hadden Street, corn markets were held, and also the Feeing Markets for farm-workers which, till 1937, took place on the second Fridays of May and November, known as "Muckle Fridays" or Term Days.

New Market before demolition

Prominently located on Nigg Kirk Road stands the church of Nigg parish, whose area included Torry before Aberdeen enlarged its boundaries. It was built in 1829 - John Smith, Architect - and superseded the ancient kirk of Saint Fittick at the Bay of Nigg. Smith's design has the bleakness of the early 19th century Perpendicular Gothic style, with a rectangular plan and a spireless tower facing the road, on the opposite side of which stands the contemporary Manse, designed by John Smith and now containing flats.

NORTH KIRK

The North Kirk in King Street is a large Grecian-style edifice – no longer used as a church, it was built in 1829-30. The main entrance – an imposing portico of four Ionic columns, is surmounted by the lofty tower, its lower portion square in plan with a clock on each side. Above this is the cylindrical top stage supported by ¾ columns and having a moulded roof surrounded by Greek antefixa ornamentation. The design of this upper part is based on the Athenian structure known as the Choragic Monument of Lysicrates. Constructed in ashlar granite masonry, the exterior is both impressive and elegant; the first of John Smith's classical designs. The interior – now converted into an arts centre – consisted of a large galleried hall with spacious stairs and vestibule.

By the mid-18th century Aberdeen burgh council had decided that a pier was necessary to check the silting-up of the Dee mouth and keep open the shipping channel. Between 1775 and 1781 the original North Pier was built to a length of 1200 ft. (360M.), the engineer being John Smeaton.

John Gibb - appointed Superintendent of Harbour Works in 1809 - supervised in 1816 the extension of the Pier by 900 ft (270M.), along with the little Abercrombie Jetty; the design was by Thomas Telford. About the same time - between 1812 and 1816 - the first South Breakwater was constructed, also by John Gibb, Engineer.

The North Pier, extended again in 1879, is now 2600 ft. - 780M. - long, and is a favourite walk to the small lighthouse at the sea end. At the Fitty end is the Round House - Pilot's Office and Customs Watch-house - dating from 1858.

OLD ADVOCATES HALL

Situated on the corner of Union Street and Back Wynd, this handsome classical building was designed in granite by John Smith, City Architect, in 1837, as the meeting-place of the Faculty of Advocates (lawyers). It is of three storeys in height with Ionic columns on the corner above the projecting balcony at first floor level, the side facing Back Wynd having pilasters and pediment over. After the advocates moved to a new hall (1869) in Concert Court, this older building was altered by A. Marshall Mackenzie, Architect, in 1898, to become a restaurant known as the Queen's Rooms; later re-furbished about 1910, it became the Queen's Cinema, now disused and unoccupied.

Huntly Street was laid out in 1818 to plans by John Smith, Architect, who intended a square – Huntly Place – to be formed on the north-east. Smith was the designer of the plain classical building, the old Blind Asylum (Nos. 50-56 Huntly Street) built in 1843; a two-storey granite structure, it is H-shaped in plan, with its central entrance surmounted at eaves height by a simple block pediment. In 1972 it ceased to be occupied as the workshops for the blind, and was converted into offices in 1978.

OLD CATHOLIC SCHOOL

Originally St Peter's Roman Catholic School – Nos. 62-86 Constitution Street – this good classic-style building was founded, and largely funded, by Father Charles "Priest" Gordon who died in 1856. The school was built, as dated, in 1833 – John Smith, Architect. The central single-storey block has, on the frieze under the pediment, the Latin motto: "Religioni et Bonis Moribus" – For Religion and Good Morals; and two small double-storey side wings are connected to the central block by porches with Roman Doric columns. Closed down as a school in 1937, it is now in a neglected state, but is to be converted into a community centre.

A handsome symmetrically facaded three-storey building, No. 35 Regent Quay was originally a laird's town-house, but is now government offices. Interesting features include moulded chimney copes, small windows in gables, double roofs, a bold projecting eaves-course and the main doorway's moulded jambs under a fine pediment - a detail in the style of the architect James Gibbs - with a flight of steps and iron railings. The house was built of Loanhead granite about the year 1772 by a Jacobite laird James Gordon of Cobairdy who died a year later. The interesting gilded sun sign on the front door pediment indicates that Gordon insured his town-house with the Sun Fire Office. In 1774 it became the offices of the Collector of Customs - the original customs house having been in the Shiprow.

Apart from Sir George Skene's Mansion, this, until its demolition about 1968, had been the only building to have survived the Guestrow clearance of the early 1930s. It stood on the west side of Barnett's Close (Map Ref. 94170641) and became the Aberdeen Dispensary – first instituted 1781 – from 1870 when a wing was added to the original house to make it L-shaped; latterly it was a clinic and offices. Dating from the 18th century the house had belonged to the family of Black of Cloghill about 1790, and after to Provost John Abercrombie. It was much altered by adding extra windows and chimneys, and roof dormers; of the old exterior of plain coursed granite masonry, the windows with chamfered jambs remained, with small-paned sashes. Skewputts were of the late type.

The old rectangular tree-lined walled garden survived until the mid-1960s, sloping down to the site of the Flour Mill, which, until its removal about 1865, was powered by the Flourmill Burn from the Loch; many other Guestrow properties had these gardens from medieval and later times.

Situated among trees, this little mansion, No. 70 Prospect Terrace - Map Ref. 94060491 - is simple in proportion, built of coursed granite, and the windows have raised architraves. It dates from before 1773 and is of one storey with basement; the entrance porch is in Neo-Greek style, a later addition with the roof dormers. Originally known as Ferryhill Cottage, it was the residence of the Abernethy family, owners of the Ferryhill Foundry and Ironworks just upstream of the Wellington Suspension Bridge.

Ferryhill derives its name from the one-time ferry across the Dee at Craiglug, where the older suspension bridge and the new concrete bridge are today.

OLD GRAMMAR SCHOOL

An inscribed granite tablet built into the wall of the former Art School, just east of the entrance gates to Robert Gordon's College, recalls the site - Map Ref. 93950636 - of the Old Grammar School of Aberdeen which is said to have been founded by the Black Friars before 1262; it was mentioned in records in 1418 when it appears to have been in the eastmost part of the grounds of the Dominican Friary. Schoolhill dates from the 15th century and takes its name either from this medieval school or from the Sang Schule for choir boys which occupied a building at the north-west corner - Map Ref. 94030633 - of St Nicholas kirkyard from at least 1475 until discontinued about 1750.

The Old School erected in 1758 was a plain single-storey building with two front wings; it superseded an earlier school built further east by master-mason George Anderson about 1624. When the 1758 building was demolished around 1880, the central portion and doorway surmounted by a pediment, with bellcote and bell dated 1625 by John Mowat of Old Aberdeen, was rebuilt at the back (north side) of the present Grammar School - a Victorian Neo-Baronial building of 1863, fronting Carden Place.

Only some ruined walls remain of this mill - Map Ref. 88510636 ; it was built by Aberdeen Burgh Council in 1616. The nearby Den of Maidencraig, between the Old Skene Road and the present A944 roadway, is a little-known and almost inaccessible beauty spot, with the tumbling Den Burn, old trees and steep fern-covered stony bluffs ; the den is divided by a rocky outcrop, a ridge with the burn on its north side. Traces of the old mill dam are still to be seen some 150 yards (135M.) west of the mill ruins. The burgh sold the meal-mill of Maidencraig in 1786, and in 1885 it was burned down and later became a ruin. In the 17th century this building was also known as the Den Mylne and the New Mill, the original Old Mill having been, at an earlier date, located where now stands Woodend or Oldmill Hospital.

OLD NIGG MANSE

Near to, and west of the ruined St Fittick's Kirk stood the 18th century Manse – Map Ref. 96210499. A two-storey house, it had a central gablet with window above the entrance door; the gablet and main house gables had curved skewputts. The stonework was granite with the east gable harled, and there were wee windows on each gable. The back wing, a later addition with a pyramid roof, was somewhat higher than that of the main roof, which had stone ridging. The last minister to occupy the old manse was Dr. David Cruden (1746-1826) parish minister for 57 years; his brother, Alexander Cruden was Provost of Aberdeen. Adjacent to the manse was a range of buildings, steading, stabling and outhouses, recalling the era when the minister worked his glebe as a farm. After a new manse, now flats, was built near the 1829 Nigg Parish Church on Kirkhill, this old manse became a private dwelling. House, outbuildings and walled garden area were all cleared away in 1965.

A three-storey building, Nos 5-9 Market Street was designed by Archibald Simpson, Architect, in 1842 as Aberdeen's Post Office after the introduction of the penny postage in 1840. The ground floor frontage was originally arcaded but alterations here and additions at roof level spoiled the facade when the building was converted to shops and offices. After demolition in 1983, the site was used for an extension to an enlarged department store fronting Union Street.

In 1875 a larger GPO was built, on the site of the former Fish Market at the corner of Market Street and Shiprow. The present Crown Street GPO, an impressive granite baronial edifice, was designed by James Cumming Wynnes, Architect, and was completed in 1906; it occupies the site of Crown Place, a terrace of two-storey houses.

OLD ROYAL INFIRMARY

The first infirmary building at Woolmanhill was built in 1741; however this was demolished and replaced, between 1832 and 1839, by what is now the south block, designed by Archibald Simpson, Architect. The Old Infirmary is one of his most successful architectural projects; it is three storeys high, the central portion having a row of six pilasters surmounted by a pediment above eaves level. The roof has a low dome, and projecting wings form a frontage of finely balanced proportions. Later additions to the north were completed in 1892 by William and John Smith, and Kelly, Architects.

South of Woolmanhill and overlooking the howe of the Den Burn was the little hill of St. John; now gone, in medieval times it was associated with the nearby Black Friars whose kirk was dedicated to that saint.

In 1828 the original town parish - St Nicholas - was divided into six parishes. One of these, South Parish, used as its first church an old Relief Presbytery chapel built in 1791 at the corner of Little Belmont Street. After the demolition of this building, its site was occupied in 1831 by a new South Kirk, designed by the City Architect John Smith. The church, Neo-Perpendicular Gothic in style and T-shaped in plan, with a tower fronting Belmont Street, is now used as a church meeting hall. Gaelic Lane, on the south side of the building, is so-called because a chapel for services in Gaelic was built about 1795 on the opposite side of the lane; this structure still exists, much altered, having been sold in 1884, and later becoming Belmont Printing Works.

The lands of Torry, in medieval times, were owned by the Abbots of Arbroath. The village became a Burgh of Barony in 1495 and remained separate until incorporated into Aberdeen City in 1891. The wee fishing community of Old Torry - Map Ref. 953053 - consisted of parallel closes and rows of cottages west of Torry Harbour and between the Dee and the leading lights (built 1842) on Sinclair Road. There were houses of 18th century and mid-19th century date in Fore Close, Sinclair Row, Pierhead and Ferry Place and Road, at the foot of which stood Petrie's Inn on the south side of the old ferry which plied across the harbour mouth until discontinued in the 1930s. The inn was demolished when the river was widened between 1869 and 1873. The fisher rows of Old Torry, single and two-storey houses, some with fore-stairs, and roofed with slates and red pantiles, were built to a characteristic layout typical of the older fishing villages of East Scotland. The rows of Old Torry were all swept away in 1972 to be replaced by industrial buildings.

Fore Close

Replacing a wooden bridge of 1541, the Pack Brig was built in 1693-4 to span the Pot or Ruthrieston burn above its junction with the Dee; it carried the Hardgate – the old south road – leading to the Bridge of Dee. Like the other Scottish pack brigs, it was built without parapets to allow pack-horses with their laden side-loads to cross easily. On its removal in 1923 to its present position 35 yards (31M.) east of its original site, it was rebuilt with stepped parapets, thus destroying its original appearance and character. The coat-of-arms panel of Robert Cruikshank of Banchory, Provost when the brig was built, was inset on the south side, but this, and other heraldic panels are now almost indecipherable.

The Pack Brig around 1920

PATAGONIAN COURT

One of Aberdeen's most picturesque old closes, this court leads from Belmont Street opposite Gaelic Lane down to the Lower Denburn by steep flights of steps and cobbled slopes. It was originally part of a lane, dating from before 1780, which led from Back Wynd to the Denburn haugh. Its exotic name could derive from the possibility that adjoining properties had connections with the late 18th century trade between the port of Aberdeen and South America and Patagonia.

Until its unwarranted destruction in 1976, this was a large earthwork mound - a Scheduled Ancient Monument - and an important example in the North-East of Scotland of a medieval motte-and-bailey castle. Situated just east of Norwood House hotel - Map Ref. 91050298 - the top of the motte was approximately 30ft. (9M.) in diameter, and here stood the earliest castle of Pitfodels, a timber tower of the De Moravia family who owned the lands from the 1300s until the late 14th century when Badfodalis or Pitfodels passed to the Reids, whose heiress Mariote married Thomas Menzies before 1542. Menzies Castle was probably a stone towerhouse, of which no trace remains, built on the original bailey, the high mound overlooking the Dee and the old crossing of the Snab Ford, which led to another early medieval castle site - the Motehill of Banchory - on the south bank of the river. The Menzies family long controlled Aberdeen's burgh councils; their Castle of Pitfodels was ruinous by the 18th century when the influence of the family - Roman Catholics and Jacobites - had declined. John Menzies, last of his line, died in 1843.

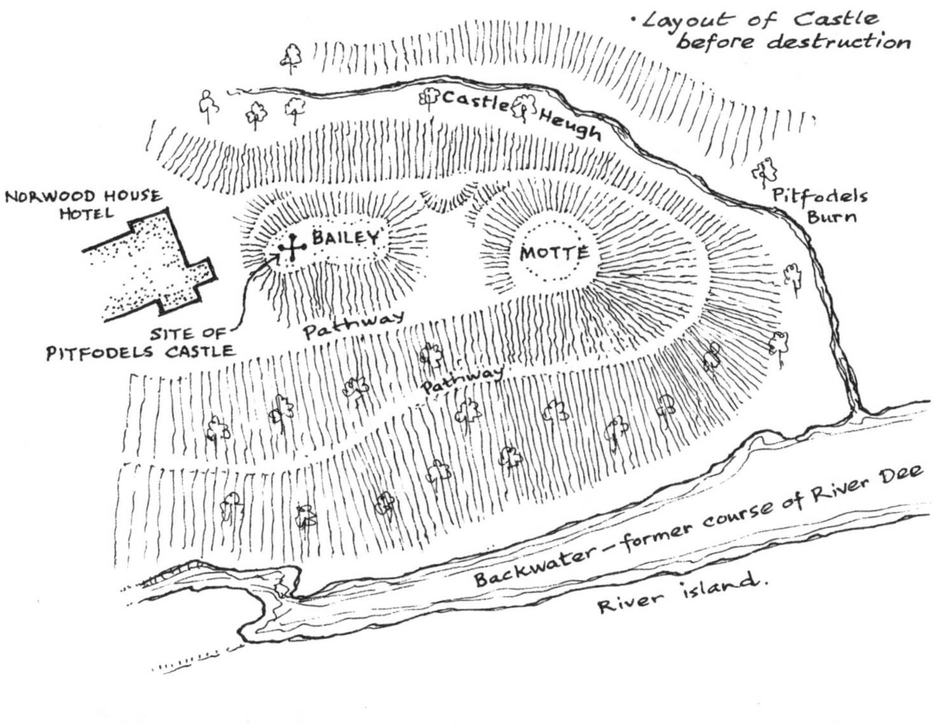

PITFODELS LODGING

Where the Aberdeen Bank building (after 1849 the Union Bank) was erected in 1801 – Architect, James Burn of Haddington – at the corner of Castle Street and Marischal Street, there stood the medieval town-house of Menzies of Pitfodels. The earliest lodging of timber was burnt down about 1530 and was rebuilt around 1535 in masonry by Thomas Menzies, Provost in 1533-4, and in 1537 when he entertained King James 5th. This toun-lodging was one of Aberdeen's first stone houses; the master-mason may have been William Jamesone, grandfather of George Jamesone, the painter. With its long garden stretching down to the shore where Virginia Street is now, this was for its time the most imposing mansion in the burgh, befitting a family which produced several provosts in the 15th and 16th centuries; in 1650 it was occupied by King Charles 2nd on his way south from his landing at Garmouth in Moray to his crowning at Scone. Until its demolition in 1800, the lodging had its 40ft. (12M.) long kitchen, with huge arched fireplace, about 10ft. (3M.) below street level; the only remnant of the building is the heraldic panel, bearing the Menzies coat-of-arms, the initials T.M. and the Royal Arms of Scotland, now preserved in Collison's Aisle, St. Nicholas Kirk. About 1740 John Menzies, 7th Laird of Pitfodels, had built, with John Adam as architect, a "back-hoose" of two storeys; it had a picturesque central gablet with ogee-moulded skew-tabling and oval oculus above three attic windows. Before its removal in 1965 this little Georgian house was approached by Victoria Court through the still existing attractive arcaded pend.

John Menzies' back-hoose from Victoria Court

Porthill - so-called because it was near the Gallowgate Port - was also known as the Windmill Hill, overlooking to the east the King's Meadow, now the West North Street area. A windmill stood from at least 1271 on a site - Map Ref. 94130684 - just east of the later factory building where a flight of steps descended past Seaview Terrace, now swept away.

The Porthill Factory, Nos. 168-172 Gallowgate - Map Ref. 9410 0684 - was, for its date, a very large building of coursed granite masonry, the block fronting the street being five storeys high; it comprised a four-sided courtyard entered, from Seamount Place, through a gateway with bell-bracket above. The entrance door of the east range was reached by a fine double-flight curved staircase of classical design. Throughout the 5-storey block the wooden floors were carried on timber beams and columns; the construction of the massive timber roof at the peinds was intricately contrived with tenoned cross-braces and diagonal ties. The factory dates from 1750-2 when the ground was feued to Alexander Livingston and Partners. "The Porthill Company" sold the factory in 1763 to Milne, Cruden and Co., who began a linen manufactory here; by 1768 it had been bought by Alexander Young. This unique and interesting industrial building was demolished in 1960, after which its site was built over by residential development.

POWIS GATE TOWERS

Dating from 1834 and erected by John Leslie of Powis with Alexander Fraser as architect, this formed the east gate and archway on College Bounds, leading formerly to the avenue to Powis House. The tall minaret-like towers have an Oriental flavour foreign to the Scottish charm of the Aulton, but nowadays they are an accepted, albeit exotic, feature of the streetscape. On both sides of the gateway, now closed to traffic, are panels bearing the coats-of-arms of the lairds of Powis.

Now in use as a community centre, this is a handsome Georgian mansion dating from 1802 - George Jaffrey, Architect. The front is harled with dressed granite masonry forming Ionic pilasters at corners. Similar pilasters frame the projecting central entrance feature, crowned by a pediment; the porch has four Roman Doric columns under a triple window with a centre arch. The estate of Powis was formerly owned by the Frasers until the heiress married a Leslie of Tullos in the Garioch. The laird who built Powis House was Hugh Leslie who succeeded in 1780 and died in 1812. In the late 19th and early 20th centuries it was the mansion of the Burnetts of Powis, until its acquisition by Aberdeen City Council in 1936.

The oldest part, the east wing – No. 51 College Bounds – facing the street, dates from 1697, and this frontage is enhanced by neat miniature iron balconies to the upper floor windows. The original house, and its restoration (1711) after a fire, was carried out by Alexander Fraser of Powis, sub-principal of Kings College – both skewputts on the street frontage are dated 1711. A panel showing the Fraser arms and the date 1697, formerly on this building and now over the moulded surround of the gateway in the wall, refers to the commencement of the original Lodge. This house was again altered in 1829, when the bow window was added to the rear wing, and in 1834 a further extension with a "minaret" tower was built.

Queen Street was laid out in 1773 and on its south side, Nº 10, built about 1775, was for a short time the boyhood home of the future Lord Byron when his mother brought him to Aberdeen in 1788; later they lived in the Broadgate after a brief stay in Virginia Street. The house was three storeys high, built of plain coursed granite, with a central window gable under a chimney-head. The round-arched pend, Chronicle Court, one of the many narrow closes connecting with Broad Street, gave access to No. 10 - the original entry a timber bolection-moulded doorway. A similar house was Nos. 35-7, on the north side; the merchant George Cruden built it in 1776-7. Nearer the eastend on the south side, Nos. 50-54, built about 1815, with arcaded ground floor doors and windows, formed a curved corner to Lodge Walk. All these properties were demolished in 1973. An earlier demolition (1969) was Nos. 39-43, a three-storey L-plan building, dating from 1776 and built by John Farquhar and William Littlejohn, Architect; they added a theatre at the back, between 1780 and 1785. On the second floor was the meeting hall of the St. Machar Freemasons Lodge. After becoming the "Aberdeen Hotel" around 1790, it was known as the Oddfellows Hall when acquired by that society.

Nº 12 Queen Street and Nº 10 — Chronicle Court

RAEDEN HOUSE

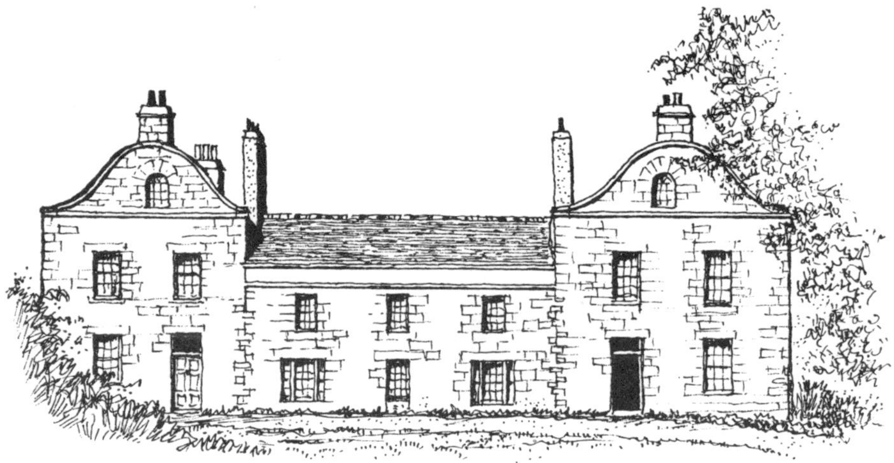

The estate of Raeden, lying between Midstocket Road - Low South Stocket Road originally - and Westburn Road, originally North Stocket Road, was feued by Alexander Dyce in 1754; he may have been the builder of the oldest central part (about 1770). In 1775 Gilbert More, merchant in Aberdeen, bought Raeden and probably added the two higher wings; their distinctive curved gables with off-centred arched windows were features similar to the Mackie Place houses and the original Gordon's Hospital. Another similarity was the roughly dressed, coursed granite masonry. Unusually there were two doorways, one in each wing, that on the south having a fine fanlight. Other interesting features were the semi-circular stair tower at the rear, and here were the "offices" and storehouses arranged round a D-shaped courtyard, approached through a pend back-entry. Gilbert More's son, George - Provost 1795-6 and 1807-8 - resided at Raeden; around 1840 it was occupied by Alexander Henderson, Advocate. This excellent Georgian mansion came into the possession of Aberdeen City Council and was demolished in 1954, the site - Map Ref. 91560665 - being now occupied by a school.

East of Raeden, before streets were laid out, was the Bonnie Moor, recalled by Bonnymuir Place; and on higher ground to the south there stood until the late 18th century the Stocket Cairn - site at Map Ref. 916064.

This vanished narrow lane - Map Ref. 94260639 - between Broad Street and Guestrow was named after Baillie Alexander Ragg who died :1719. At the south-east corner of the lane and Broad Street stood No. 35, a three-storey tenement with the unique feature of a gargoyle-like sculpture of a man's head built into the corner about 4.5M. (15 ft.) above the pavement. Very similar to the cast-iron faces found, with projecting water-pipe at the mouth on the town's old wells, this is said to have been set up by the owner George Russel (1810-1898), an eccentric who sculpted the head to spite a neighbour he did not like. Russel is also remembered by the city's police constables and the scaffies who benefit every year from the Russel Trust bequeathed by him. After the building's demolition in 1959 the gargoyle has been preserved at the south-east corner of the nearby Skene Mansion.

The 'Russel Face' on corner of Ragg's Lane

No. 33 Broad Street, three storeys high with steeply pitched roof, was removed with No. 35; it had an inscribed stone, at the south end at eaves level, with the initials K.T. and I.G., and also 1711, evidently the date of the building. On the north of Ragg's Lane Nos. 37-9 Broad Street, also demolished :1959, had upper windows with splayed jambs and the date 1741 on the south-east skewputt.

The Records Office - No.3 Castlegate - stood at the corner of Justice Street, where it was replaced by the Salvation Army Citadel in 1896. A Georgian building two storeys high with a piended roof, its symmetrical frontage had a central pediment and balustrade at eaves. It was built in 1779 as the records depository for Aberdeen city and county; the architect may have been Robert Adam who submitted a design in 1772. On the ground floor was the sherriff clerk's department and the advocates' library was above. A new record office was erected in King Street in 1833, but the older building remained until cleared away in 1891 along with the adjoining building to the south, No.5 Castlegate, which was the town-house of Francis Gordon, laird of Kincardine Oneil, from about 1800 till his death in 1861; this plain three-storey building of early 19th century date had a frontage of dressed granite.

In medieval times the Citadel site - then known as Castlesyde - was occupied by the Justiciar's Court House and the lodging of Alexander Comyn, 2nd Earl of Buchan from 1244-1289, who was the Justiciar of North Scotland from 1257 till his death.

PROVOST ROBERTSON'S HOUSE

Provost Robertson's House from Ross's Court – about 1850

Now University property, this building – Nos. 6-8 Upperkirkgate – was in 1899 rebuilt, with its doorway copied from that of the Scots College, Paris, on the site of an older house, of which the part facing the street had originally been built in 1680 by George Leslie, Provost 1685-7, and his wife Christian Walker. Of this lodging, the only remnants are the three dormer pediments – one displaying a coat-of-arms panel of the Leslie family; another inscribed G. L. and C. W.; the third dated 1680. The Provost's son, James Leslie, Advocate, sold the property to James, father of Alexander Robertson of Glascoego, Provost three times between 1740 and 1757. Robertson added the wing along the west side of Ross's Court, the pend under the older house, in 1730. Parts of this wing have been built into the present building, including the fine moulded inner arch of the pend, the corbelling of the rebuilt stair turret, and the old doorway with its inscribed lintel: "Alexander Robertson • Jean Strachan • 1730." The Robertson coat-of-arms with Latin motto "Robore et Sapore" (By Strength and Prudence) is on a panel above, the shield now very much weathered.

ROLLAND'S LODGING

Demolished in 1935, this house, originally No. 38 Castlegate - Map Ref. 94510635 - was of very considerable architectural and historic interest. Dating from the 16th century when it was the lodging of the Rollands, Masters of the Royal Mint in Exchequer Row, it was partially rebuilt and added to around 1630; in 1704 it was the property of Sir Samuel Forbes of Foveran, writer of the "Description of Aberdeenshire".

The entrance was by a central pend through to St. John's Court and the house's twin harled gables facing the street had irregularly spaced windows - a typical medieval feature. Inside there were vaulted basements and the upper rooms had arched fireplaces, wall aumbries and good pine panelling. After demolition, one round arched fireplace was built into the old Maryculter Manse, restored in 1936 - Fenton Wyness, Architect, to form the Warden's House at the City of Aberdeen Boy Scouts Camping Ground, Templars Park. The site of Rolland's Lodging is now occupied by an office building.

This three-storey harled house dates from the early 18th century, with a later Victorian extension to the west. Features of interest are the curved skew-putts and unusually low pitched dormer windows, and at the back, the piend-roofed stair tower and the semi-octagonal projecting wing with bellcast roof - a later addition. In the 1840s the House was bought by John Smith, City Architect and Superintendent of Works, who died here in 1852. Willowbank, a nearby mansion built by James Black in the late 18th century, was acquired in 1843 by Smith's son-in-law, Alexander Gibb, son of John Gibb, Engineer. Rosebank House - now Nos. 9-11 Rosebank Place - was incorporated in the north side of that street when it was laid out in 1886. Before that the grounds of the house extended to the south and east, where a walled garden sloped down to overlook the Ferryhill Mill and Dam.

Rosebank House from Willowbank

PROVOST ROSS'S HOUSE

One of the very few medieval houses remaining in Aberdeen, this building – originally Nos. 44-46 Shiprow – was typical of an important merchant's residence near the harbour. Three storeys high, with projecting gabled wing corbelled at eaves level, the house had its entrance door, with coat-of-arms panel over, in the wing; another door was approached by way of the forecourt enclosed by an ashlar masonry wall with gate to the street. Skewputts on the south-east and south-west corners have the defaced monogram RW and the date of the building – 1593. This monogram and the inscribed initials R.W. and M.C. on the gable's skew stones are believed to refer to Robert Watson, wright (whose collaborator Andrew Jamesone the master-mason may have built the house) and to his wife Margaret Collie. One of the dormer windows is dated 1593 with the initials I.M., possibly referring to John Menzies who held the superiority of the property.

The building passed through the ownership of several occupants in the 17th century until in 1702 it was bought by John Ross of Arnage, merchant, who was Provost 1710-11. By the mid-20th century the house had become neglected and a near ruin, but demolition by the City Council was prevented by the National Trust, now owners, and others. In 1954 its restoration – A.G.R. Mackenzie, Architect – was completed, along with the adjoining building Nos. 48-50 Shiprow, a plainer house with an interesting entrance door and pend (originally called "Abbey Place") within a double arcade feature, the capital of the central column being inscribed T.F. and I.F. and dated 1710; there is a similar inscription on the high south-west skew table, and this date would refer to the frontage only, the older main building behind being of the 17th century.

The interiors of these two fine buildings were considerably altered to form the Aberdeen Maritime Museum in 1984.

Demolished in 1886, this mansion was sited–Map Ref. 91910565–approximately where No.50 Queen's Road stands today. Built by Arthur Forbes in 1675, the main south-facing block was a rectangular three-storey building of the "ha'-hoose" type with central doorway, originally at ground floor level, having its lintel inscribed A·1675·F ; there were corbie-step gables, moulded chimney copes and roof dormers of the old single-pitch type. Robert Forbes of Rubislaw was Provost 1671-3 ; in 1687 the estate and house were bought by Sir George Skene of Fintray. He had the later entrance built–with his coat-of-arms panel above–at first floor, reached by a fine flight of steps ; he also added the two flanking wings.

In front of the east wing was the remnant of an earlier building with vaulted basement–possibly a tower-house type of castle of the late 16th century, when Rubislaw belonged to the Rutherfords. Alexander Rutherford was Provost seven times, and in 1605 was Commissioner to the Estates.

To the north behind the house was a large walled garden with a splendid 17th century sundial, originally from the Earl Marischal's Hall in the Castlegate : now at Schivas House.

RUBISLAW QUARRY

Rubislaw Quarry, situated - Map Ref. 912054 - between Queen's Road and Anderson Drive North, began as a small hill, about 60 ft. (18M.) high in 1775, when some granite stone quarrying was started here. However in 1778 it was sold by the town council as being unlikely to produce good stone for building. In the early 1800s the Skenes of Rubislaw owned the quarry and it was leased by John Gibb (1776-1850) who realised its possibilities. Along with his son Alexander (1804-67), the civil engineer, he developed the quarry, and eventually its light bluish-grey granite provided most of the causeys or setts for the town's streets, also the building stone that made Aberdeen the "Granite City."

When the quarry was closed down in 1971, it was about 430 ft. (130M.) deep and some 800 ft. (240M.) by 400 ft. (120M.) across.

This one-storey round-ended building, now a shop (No. 34 Queen's Road), was occupied as a toll-house between 1837 and 1865, when tolls were abolished. From here Spademill Road, with its avenue of trees, leads to Spademill Lane and Rubislaw Den South; this was a section of an old cross-country route leading to the Stocket and the Old Skene Road. Where it crossed the Denburn by a stone bridge there stood, until 1880, a small cottoun of red-tiled cottages known as Hirpletillim – its site is now occupied by No. 24 Rubislaw Den South.

The name Spademill derives from the manufacturing here of the wooden spades, known also as shovels, sheels or skips, used for turning the barley in the nearby Glenburn (or Glenburnie) whisky distillery – located at Map Ref. 920058, from 1816 – when the distiller was James Dunbar – till 1857, when the then owners, Brown, Farquharson and Co., discontinued distilling. The disused buildings were leased by G.W. Wilson for photographic printing until 1875, after which date they were cleared away.

The name - meaning "Ruadri's toun" - recalls Ruadri who was Mormaer of Mar in the reign of Alexander Ist (died 1124). Ruadri, who was succeeded as Mormaer by Morgund about 1150, had set up a motehill castle which controlled both the river crossing at Foords of Dee and the route of the Old Deeside Road (now Broomhill Road) leading to Mar. This earthwork mound was sited between the south end of Ruthrieston Circle and Ruthrieston Road - Map Ref. 928041; it was removed by gravel extraction in the early 20th century. Near the ford stood the gibbet of Ruthrieston until the 17th century. The little community at the west end of the Bridge of Dee became important agriculturally; its market stance, where the house Fordbank now stands, continued to be the location for horse and cattle markets on the third Monday of every month until about 1880. Another market, the Mannofield Tryst was held about ¾ mile (650M.) to the west on the second Monday each month. Near Margaret Place - where only one old cottage remains - was a cot-toun of lax (salmon) fishers, and one of the few surviving old buildings of the Cot-toun of Ruthrieston is No. 571 Holburn Street, a plain two-storey granite house, now much altered but originally the "Museum Inn" close to the market stance. The inn was so-called because around 1850 its proprietor kept a collection of byegones and antiquities.

Nº 571 Holburn Street

Archibald Simpson's first public building was St. Andrew's Episcopal Chapel in King Street: since 1914 the Cathedral Church of the Diocese of Aberdeen and Orkney. Built in 1817 in a rather severe style of Neo-Perpendicular Gothic, the masonry is Craigleith sandstone, a departure from the local granite which Simpson made famous. Unusually for such an important church there is no tower; the chancel was designed in 1880 by George Edmund Street, Architect, and the plain entrance porch on the King Street frontage was added (1911) by Sir Robert Lorimer, Architect. The interior was re-decorated between 1934 and 1943 as a memorial to Dr. Samuel Seabury-consecrated (1784) in Aberdeen as the first Bishop of the American Episcopal Church. The vaulted side aisles were at this time very beautifully decorated with the coats-of-arms of local families and of 48 of the United States. The Renaissance-type ciborium and high altar also date from this time; the architect for the whole scheme was the famous Aberdeen-born church architect Sir Ninian Comper (1864-1960). There is a fine marble statue sculpted by John Flaxman, of Bishop John Skinner, Primus of the Episcopal Church, who, after a priesthood of 42 years, died in 1816, while St Andrews was being built.

ST. CLEMENT'S KIRK

Facing St Clement Street, this church building is on the site of an early medieval chapel, believed to have been dedicated to St Fotin. In 1498 a later chapel - of St Clement - was founded for the fishing community of Fitty. It became ruinous after the Reformation, being restored in 1631 and again in 1700. The graveyard, containing many old tombstones, was enclosed by a boundary dyke which, as stated on an inscribed sandstone panel, recently restored, and built in north-east of the entry gates, was put up by George Davidson of Pettens in 1650. The church was rebuilt in 1788 after the demolition of the medieval kirk.

When St. Clement's became a separate parish from St. Nicholas in 1828, the present granite building was erected in the Neo-Perpendicular Gothic style - John Smith, Architect; its appearance has suffered from the removal, during 1972, of the pinnacles and balustrading on top of the square tower.

Another medieval religious building at or near Fitty was St Anne's hospital for poor women, to which a chapel was added by Alexander Galloway in 1519; these buildings still existed at the Reformation, but the exact site is now unknown.

· George Davidson's Stone Panel ·

Overlooking the Bay of Nigg on the west side of St. Fittick's Road, this ruined church within its old graveyard is now surrounded by a bleak "recreation" area where once were farm parks. Believed to occupy the site of a chapel dedicated to the 7th century Irish St. Fiakre, the church was consecrated by David de Bernham, Bishop of St. Andrews in 1242; at this time it formed, with the nearby timber castle on Balnagask motehill, the feudal centre of the lands and parish of Nigg. The building, rectangular in plan, is mostly 17th century in date, incorporating the pre-Reformation kirk, with traces of a "leper" window. The east gable's once handsome bellcote - now very dilapidated - was dated 1704 with the initials of the then minister Richard Maitland, and above is the weathervane dated 1763; the bell dated 1759 was by John Mowat of Aberdeen. In the north-east of the walled kirkyard with its many old tombstones is a small anti-bodysnatcher Watch House, built in the 1820s - now unroofed.

St. Fittick's Well, originally located on the south-east shore of the Bay of Nigg - Map Ref. 965046 - is now lost due to erosion by the sea. It was renowned for its curative properties and on St Fittick's Day (30th August) and on May Day, pilgrimages were made to drink at the circular basin of the holy well; it was also a "rag" well where pieces of cloth were left as offerings - a survival of pagan rituals, involving the veneration of wells and water which dated back to the pre-Celtic Iron Age of about 2500 years ago.

ST. JOHN'S WELL

One of Aberdeen's oldest wells, this was originally situated just west of where the Summer Road (now Summer Street), leading from the Crabstane on Hardgate over to Upper Denburn, descended to a brig built (1754) across the Denburn where Rosemount Viaduct is now - Map Ref. 935064. It was so-called because the Knights of St John of Jerusalem are said to have owned a croft here in the Middle Ages. The well, supplying water to the folk of Gilcomston, was rebuilt in 1852, the lintel being inscribed in Latin: SANCTI JOANNIS FONS. AB OPERUM PUBLICORUM CURATORIBUS REFECTUS. A.D. MDCCCLII - meaning: St. John's Well. Renovated by the Supervisors of Public Works. 1852. In 1885 the construction of the Viaduct involved the removal of the old well; it was built in under the flight of granite steps which replaced the steep brae of the Summer Road down to the east end of Skene Row and Hardweird. After the demolition of those streets in the 1930s, the well remained, although neglected and almost covered by debris, until in 1955 it was re-erected, complete with its Loanhead granite ashlar surround, inscribed lintel, side walls and steps down, in front of the Order of St. John headquarters building at No. 28 Albyn Place.

The site of this chapel - Map Ref. 943062 - was approximately where, at No. 28 Adelphi, the former close St Catherine's Court, led through to a pend at No. 32 Shiprow, long demolished. The chapel, dedicated to St. Katherine of Siena, is said to have been founded in 1242 by John Kennedy of Kermuck, Constable of Aberdeen Castle. In ruins by 1660 it occupied the top of St. Katherine's Hill, a prominent height within the medieval burgh sloping down all round to the Netherkirkgate on the north, to Putachieside to the west and to Shiprow on the east and south. St Catherine's Wynd, off Union Street, once linked Netherkirkgate with the top of the Shiprow. The only remnants of the chapel are a very weathered red sandstone grave-slab, of 15th century date, built into a north boundary wall behind No. 24 Adelphi; and the baptismal font - said to be in a local garden.

St Katherine's Hill was reduced in height when Union Street was laid out, and later levelled further when the Adelphi was built about 1810. Of the Adelphi buildings, No. 21, originally within a court, was occupied by the papermaking family of Pirie in the 1840s; a handsome harled house with a good entrance door and front steps, it was gutted by fire in 1970.

Coat-of-Arms of Kennedys of Kermuck Constables of the Castle of Aberdeen

ST. MACHAR'S CATHEDRAL KIRK

The earliest kirk at or near the present Cathedral in the Chanonry dated from Pictish times and was founded by the Irish St Machar (Mochreibha) about AD 580. King David 1st endowed the See of Aberdeen around 1130 and it's first bishop was Nechtan, transferred from the old Culdee monastery of Mortlach, a foundation of St Moluag. The Cathedral was also the kirk of the parish of St Machar; the Aulton originally was the Kirkton of Seaton. Between 1170 and 1190 a church in the Romanesque-Transitional style was begun; of this only a part of one pier remains. Bishop Henry Cheyne, around the year 1286 began a new Choir in Early Gothic style; it was completed by 1345. The piers under the crossing and parts of the nave and south transept walling are remnants of Bishop Alexander Kyninmond the 2nd's work, in Decorated Gothic-built about 1366. The main part of the present church building, including the Nave, the excellent Late Gothic north transept (St John's Aisle) and the impressive castellated west towers were built in granite masonry in the time of Henry de Lichtoun, bishop between 1423 and 1440. The able statesman-bishop William Elphinstone completed the central tower and its lead-covered timber spire around 1512. His successor Gavin Dunbar finished the twin west steeples in freestone, and also the south transept (Dunbar's Aisle), by the year 1530; his finely carved tomb is in the south wall of his aisle. The Nave has a most notable heraldic oak ceiling, with coat-of-arms panels of the European monarchs, Scottish nobles and bishops: constructed by James Winter, an Angus architect-builder, about 1520. After the Reformation neglect and vandalism caused the ruin and collapse of the central tower and choir in 1688.

The Cathedral Kirk is scheduled as an Ancient Monument. The graveyard, with tombs as early as the 16th century, is enclosed by 18th century walls; the gate-lodges in ashlar granite were designed by John Smith, Architect (1832).

The location of this well was between Marywell Street and Affleck Street – Map Ref. 9405; in the Middle Ages this area was the Well Croft, or Lady Croft, that is, the croft of Our Lady, St Mary. After 1809 the Incorporated Trade of Shoemakers laid out St. Mary's Place and Marywell Street, whose names derive from the old well which became filled up and built over.

Other wells and springs existed between South College Street and Springbank, hence the name; one well 20ft (6M.) deep was uncovered behind No. 69 Dee Street, an interesting house of the 1820s, with a Roman Doric columned porch. Other good granite houses of the same period include No. 43 Dee Street and "Springbank" (No. 18 Dee Place). Behind the latter is the Old Mill Road now a narrow lane which can be walked from Marywell Street across Crown and Dee Streets to descend eventually to Union Glen. This old route originally led from the burgh to the Ferryhill Mill which existed in 1667, being situated on the west side of Albury Road – Map Ref. 936054 – opposite Albury Bowling Club; the mill-dam, to the west, had been fed by a lade from the How Burn.

• 'Springbank' – Nº 18 Dee Place •

The two Kirks of St. Nicholas about 1830

The medieval Town Kirk of St Nicholas is first referred to in a papal "bulla" of 1157, but it is likely that an earlier church stood here, perhaps dedicated to St. Ninian, or to one of his Pictish missionaries; a stone 500mm. by 200mm (20ins. by 8ins.) with inscribed cross of the Early Christian type was found in the church ruins after the destructive fire of 1874. An early religious foundation on such a site overlooking the Dark Age fishing community on the Dee estuary is possibly the reason for the later Burgh Kirk being located outside the town's ports and defences.

The oldest parts of the medieval cruciform kirk to survive are the late 12th century Romanesque arched crossing and pillars, and the interiors of the aisles (transepts). Sub-floor excavations in 1974 confirmed the approximate date of building of transepts and crossing. The Aisle of the Haly Blude (North Transept) has a traceried window (1518) and was renamed Collison's Aisle after 1594. The South Transept or Drum's Aisle - burial place of the Irvines of Drum - was substantially altered in 1837. The Nave was restored in 1357, the Choir was rebuilt 1477-98, and a lead-covered oaken spire erected in 1513. After the Reformation, when St Nicholas was the largest parish kirk in Scotland, the carved rood screen was replaced by a stone partition (1596). The Nave became the Auld or Town Kirk, the Choir becoming the New or East Kirk which stood until its rebuilding in granite in the Gothic Revival style in 1837 - Archibald Simpson, Architect. The disastrous fire of 1874 wrecked both central spire and Simpson's Kirk, which, with a new larger steeple in granite, was restored by William Smith, Architect, between 1875-77.

One of the most impressive features of Union Street's architecture is this facade, designed by John Smith in 1830; it consists of a high Ionic columnar screen in granite along the south boundary of the burial ground which did not originally extend so far south, but was enlarged about 1820. In the centre is a high round arch with entablature flanked on each side by double columns. Each wing contains six smaller-proportioned columns linked by ornamental railings, with pylon-type end blocks.

The cemetery is enclosed on the Back Wynd side by a high 17th century rubble wall with mural memorials, some in the Baroque style of the late 1600s. Later tombs include many of local families, and provosts, ministers, doctors, architects and engineers. Most prominent is the Greek Doric style monument to Dr Robert Hamilton, University professor and economist; the design was by John Smith (1833).

Dating from 1822, probably to a design by John Smith, City Architect, this simple building, No. 55A St Nicholas Street – Map Ref. 94100635 – was demolished, with the adjoining properties in 1983. A plain classical frontage, in Rubislaw granite, with pediment over, originally formed the gateway entrance to the Town Kirkyard from St Nicholas Street, the entry leading through the opening up three separate flights of steps to the burial ground. The upper floor under the pediment housed the gatekeeper's accommodation; in 1878 the building was converted into a shop.

The west side of St Nicholas Street, laid out 1805-7, was on the line of an earlier lane, the narrow Dubbie Raw, leading from the Netherkirkgate to Schoolhill, beyond which northwards, George Street was laid out in about 1790, the section as far as Loch Street being known as Tannery Lane from 1764.

Originally the nave of the medieval parish church, the West Kirk, known as the Auld or Toun Kirk after the Reformation, became ruinous by 1732; it was used as stables by Cumberland's dragoons in 1746. The medieval nave was about 17ft. (5M.) longer than the present West Kirk designed in 1741 by James Gibbs (1682-1754) the Aberdeen-born architect whose notable career included many splendid buildings throughout England, but only two or three in Scotland. This church building is in the Renaissance style with pedimented west gable and arched doorway, and arcaded side windows. It was built, of Craigleith freestone, between 1752-5 : James Wylie, Master-mason. The interior has a barrel-vaulted roof, groin-vaulted side aisles, and arcades carried on heavy piers. The pulpit and oak gallery fronts are as originally designed, with a grandiose canopy over the Lord Provost's pew; the Toun Kirk is used for the "Kirkin' of the Council". The church contains the beautiful needlework panels sewn in 1660 by Mary Jamesone, daughter of the artist George Jamesone.

West Gable

ST. PAUL'S GATEWAY

A finely proportioned Renaissance-style round arched gateway, with rusticated Roman Doric pilasters and bold cornice, led on through a wide pend to Chapel Court and St Paul's Episcopal Church, the second church on this site. The archway with its iron gates was part of an early 18th century tenement, Nos. 53-7 Gallowgate, and dated from 1721. The first Episcopalian chapel also dated from this time; it was built in early Georgian style and the designer was possibly Alexander Jaffrey of Kingswells, Quaker and architect. A north wing or aisle was added in 1764 by the architect William Littlejohn, who laid out Littlejohn Street (originally East Street) and parts of Queen and Marischal Streets.

St Paul's Chapel was demolished and replaced in 1865 by a Gothic Revival church – it was, with tenements and gateway, all swept away in 1986.

Situated between King Street and the Spital is St Peter's Cemetery, and within the bounds of the original kirkyard are the foundations of St Peter's Kirk. Nearby to the south-west stood the Hospital or "Spital" founded in the late 12th century for the poor and infirm by Matthew Kyninmond, Bishop of Aberdeen 1172-1199; his hospital was dedicated to St Peter. In 1427 a chapel, later known as St Peter's, was built in accordance with a charter granted by Bishop Henry de Lichtoun; this became the kirk of the parish of Spital and the hospital continued to care for the sick till at least 1541. The kirk foundations, much overgrown and the area filled with burials, measure about 66 by 24 ft. (20M. by 7M.). At the east end is the walled burial enclosure – a simple Grecian-style building 24 by 21 ft. (7 by 6M.) of about 1840 – of the family of Moir of Scotstown and Spital; their coat-of-arms, three Moors' heads on a bronze plaque were once over the entrance. The arched gateway to the cemetery at St Peter's Gate has still this coat-of-arms in bronze above the arch with the Latin motto: "Non sibi sed cunctis" – Not for oneself but for all.

The east side of the street called Spital has been much rebuilt but some interesting 18th century houses remain, in particular on the west side, where Nos. 45 and 49 stand back with their access up steps, through gates flanked by square granite pillars topped with ball finials. No. 49 has its door in a symmetrical gable with curved skewputts and wee windows – features reminiscent of late medieval work.

Remains of St. Peter's Kirk and Moir Mausoleum.

SEATON HOUSE

Once situated in Seaton Park near the banks of the Don - Map Ref. 939092 - this large and stately two-storey mansion house was demolished in 1963, after destruction by fire, having been acquired by Aberdeen City Council in 1947; previous owners had been the Hay family since 1829. The house was of three periods. The oldest portions, in the north-west wing, dating from the mid-17th century, were built by James Gordon, a baillie of Old Aberdeen in 1661, who died 1714. The most interesting part was the south block, built of brickwork with dressed work in sandstone, the piended roof slated; the main entrance doorway in the central section under the pediment and three-light window was grand classical architecture. It was built around 1715 for Gordon's son-in-law, Colonel John Middleton M.P. for the Aberdeen Burghs, and the architect was possibly Middleton's friend the Aberdeen-born James Gibbs. The north-east wing was early 19th century in date.

The surrounding grounds, now the Park, included the stables of about 1750 and the mid-18th century walled garden within its high "Scotch Bond" brick dykes. On the wooded bank above the scenic riverside path along the Don is the now-neglected "Maiden's Well" - Map Ref. 93750943 - also called Lady James Hay's Well, as inscribed with date 1861, the year of her death.

Now called Don Street, this thoroughfare - the gait or way to Seaton - leads from Old Aberdeen Town-House to the Brig o' Balgownie. Despite alterations and restorations, it remains a picturesque street with many examples of good Scots vernacular architecture.

On the west side No. 23 Don Street is 18th century in date: restored in 1939 - Dr. William Kelly, Architect. No. 45 is an early 19th century house with a Doric columned porch; No. 49 "The Close" also dates from the early 1800s. The last buildings on this side are a row of single-storey cottages, Nos. 113-119 Don Street, with slated roofs, except one red-pantiled; all have undergone modernisation but these granite houses are early 19th century in date. Outside No. 119 at the edge of the pavement there stood, until around 1950 one of the few street wells - long out of use - remaining in the Aulton.

Seatongate · Nos 113-9 Don Street · before alterations.

Nos 60-64 Shiprow

The Shiprow is first mentioned in records in 1281, and the 17th century site of its port or gateway, dating from at least 1443, was where the street narrowed just west of Shore Brae - Map Ref. 94310612. It was also known as the Trinity Port in the 17th century when it led to the old Trinity Hall to the west.

Within the town gate on the north side at Nos. 60-64 Shiprow stood an early 16th century building, now much altered and reduced in height, the present structure incorporating the lower front stone wall with two narrow weapon-slits, and a doorway with Gothic pointed moulded arch leading to the interior which has remains of barrel-vaulting on the inside of the north wall. Externally there is a splay-back at first floor level, indicating that the house was probably three storeys high. This is the oldest stone structure in the street and the remnant suggests a building of some importance, either a laird's lodging or possibly one of the two Shiprow tenements or properties recorded as owned by the Knights Templars before 1312, when they passed to the Hospitallers of St. John until the Reformation. On the east side of this building is a very fine classical-style granite round archway, rebuilt here in 1965, but evidently taken from a building of the late 17th century.

A short street, this led down from the Shiprow to the harbour but has almost been obliterated due to new road alignments. In 1974 excavations uncovered two lengths of the early 15th century stone-built harbour wall, about 3ft (1M.) wide, under the foundations of a 19th century warehouse on the west corner of Shore Brae and Trinity Quay. This pier, known as the Quayhead in the 17th century, stretched along the south part of the west side of the Brae and was the mooring for unloading ships in the Middle Ages until 1623; then it was covered over and the old harbour infilled by reclamation to form the Shorelands below the Castlehill, and the New Pier – now Trinity and Regent Quays – was built. At the top of Shore Brae the Trinity Congregational Church building occupies the site, until its demolition in 1876, of a high three-storey house of late 17th century date. Its harled frontage, with roll-moulded surrounds to the main door and windows, large dormer gablets with skewputts, the plain skews above round corners corbelled below eaves, and the small paned windows symmetrically arranged, all indicated that this building was one of the earliest classical-style town-houses in Aberdeen. A square carved cartouche panel above the door gave the date of building as 1692, with initials I.S. and C.E., evidently referring to the owner and his wife. The wee door and basement windows were probably Victorian alterations, while the protruding stone tusks indicated that here may have stood the later Shiprow Port, called also the Quayhead Port as it defended the Shore; this gateway, sited west of Shore Brae until after mid-17th century, could have been re-positioned higher up the street where it survived until its removal in the 1770s.

View of house dated 1692 – before demolition.

SIR GEORGE SKENE'S MANSION

Restored by the City Council (1953) - E. Meldrum, Architect, as a period museum this mansion, once one of the west side properties of the now vanished Guestrow, is a first-class example of a Scottish town-house. It is built mainly of unquarried granite stones; dressed work is of freestone. The oldest parts dating from 1545 are the ground floor vaults and paved first floor where there is a fine medieval fireplace. The earliest owners were a burgess family named Knollis or Knox. From 1610-15 it was the residence of Peter Blackburn, the Episcopalian Bishop of Aberdeen. Baillie Matthew Lumsden added the west wing in 1626 - the top floor contains an excellent example of an early 17th century tempera-painted ceiling decorated with scenes from the time of Christ. George Skene, prosperous merchant and landowner - Provost 1676-85, and knighted by King James 7th in 1681 - practically rebuilt the main house, including the main stair tower, turrets, corner sundial, and flat roof - an unusual feature in that era - after he acquired it in 1669. The panelled rooms and very ornate plaster ceilings were done at this time, as was the finely carved "Restoration-motif" entrance doorway, lintel and Skene coat-of-arms panel with motto "Gratis a Deo data" - Thanks be given to God. The flat lead roofing has been relaid, and a part of the interesting timber roof structure of beams and purlins remains. Cumberland billetted himself in this house for six weeks in 1746 on his way to Culloden. A booklet is available, describing the interior of the building, now unhappily overwhelmed by the multi-storey block built in 1970 for local authority offices.

Dating from the 1820s this part of Skene Street originally consisted of four terraced houses of two storeys with basement and attics, built of good granite ashlar masonry. The symmetrical Georgian frontage is centred on the double entrance doorway with arched fanlight; above at eaves level there is a blocking course and panel lettered "Skene Place". Restored in 1982 to form 12 flats, the Victorian roof dormers were replaced by skylights; the terrace is now a splendid example of elegant yet simple-proportioned domestic street architecture.

SKENE TERRACE

During the 1820s this was called Chapel Street as it led from the Denburn to Gilcomston Chapel of Ease. The west side of the street dating from around 1800 includes Nos. 40-52, and these seven houses form a most interesting two-storeyed terraced group with basements – a good design solution to the problem of stepped buildings on a downhill-sloping street. The entrance doors of Nos. 40-44 are approached by flights of steps, No. 44 having a round-arched doorway. Nos. 48-50 has a projecting flat-roofed entrance canopy supported by four Tuscan columns. The original iron railings at steps and basements have been retained, and uniformity of design is partly achieved by good proportion; however alterations to windows and the various ugly roof dormers detract from the overall attractiveness.

Located behind the west side of College Bounds, this wee secluded graveyard with its few tombs marks the site - Map Ref. 93900800 - of the Snow Parish Kirk founded in 1498 by Bishop William Elphinstone. The dedication to St Mary ad Nives - Our Lady of the Snows - has been explained by its being named by the Bishop after the Roman basilican church of Santa Maria Maggiore, the site of which is said to have been indicated by a miraculous and unseasonal snow fall in August. Though intended to serve the Aulton, the kirk was annexed in 1499 by King James 4th to the King's College. The kirk was similar in plan to, but much smaller than the College Chapel; a simple nave with apsidal chancel - the dimensions are about 80 by 30 feet (24 by 9 M.). After 1640 it was roofless and became ruinous. Its burial ground was divided among adjoining owners and the present enclosure is actually the area occupied by the kirk, the surrounding wall - of the local Seaton brick - being on top of the old foundations. After the Reformation this became a burial place of Catholic clergy and of families such as Menzies of Pitfodels - a notable tomb is the grave-slab of Sir Gilbert Menzies who died 1669.

At No. 9 College Bounds, built into the high stone rubble wall is part of what was probably the entrance gateway to the Snow Kirk; the roll-moulded round arch remains, with a bold stringcourse above, and Bishop Elphinstone's coat-of-arms panel.

The original site of this old and noted well was at the bottom of steps down a bank on the south-west side of Spa Street - Map Ref. 93650644 - about 80ft. (24M.) from the west gable of the old Royal Infirmary. It was famed in the Middle Ages for its curative chalybeate waters and became celebrated because of a pamphlet published in 1580 by Dr Gilbert Skene, King James 6th's doctor. About 1635 when George Jamesone the painter laid out his garden, known as the Four-neukit Garden, just west of the now-underground Gilcomston Burn, he also repaired the Spa Well on the opposite bank. It was rebuilt in 1670 by Baillie Alexander Skene, and renovated by the Town Council in 1851. After the 1860s the well ceased to be used as a water supply point, and the gable of the 17th century well-house building was moved in 1893 to the infirmary side of Spa Street. In 1977 the well was re-erected, with its original flanking seats restored, in its present location adjoining the Denburn Centre development; when this was built it finally removed any remaining traces of Jamesone's square garden along with Garden-Nook Close, a lane which, until the 1960s, led from Upper Denburn. The remaining well-house, of ashlar sandstone, has a low arch with above it the thistle, rose, sun and fleur-de-lys motifs; and there are three inscriptions: the oldest is Jamesone's:- "As Heavens give me, so I give thee", and the Latin "Hoc fonte derivita salus in patriam populumque fluat" - May health derived from this spring flow to country and people; Skene's:- "Spada Rediviva. 1670" - The Spa come to life again; and at the top:- "Renovatum est opus anno MDCCCLI" - The work was renewed in the year 1851.

The Spa Well at its original location

Now demolished, this toll-house stood – Map Ref. 930032 – on the corner of an old farm roadway to Caiesdykes and Kincorth, now Cairngorm Road. It had originally been a simple single-storey thatched cottage probably of late 18th century date. Its later conversion to toll-house was due to its situation on the east side of the Aberdeen to Stonehaven turnpike road (now A92), which after around 1800 superseded the ancient medieval Causey Mounth route south by Hilldowntree, Tollohill and Haremoss ("Drumthwacket Moor") to the Mearns coast. From 1830 travellers on the turnpike had to pay tolls which were eventually abolished in 1865. This wee cottage had its roof slated and at its west gable was built a semicircular bow end with windows for the toll-keeper to observe and check passing traffic at the toll-bar across the roadway. The keeper's remuneration was very small and was often augmented by selling illicit whisky to drouthy travellers.

Shepherd's Court and No. 1 – looking towards Guestrow

Removed during the Guestrow slum clearance in 1930, this house was at No. 1 Shepherd's Court, reached through an arched gateway at No. 21 Guestrow. The entrance door was in a square tower splayed into an upper round stair tower - an unusual feature - and topped by a conical slated roof. The gateway, with its moulded sandstone round arch, was moved in 1931 to the Union Terrace Gardens, and in 1970 re-sited in front of Sir George Skene's Mansion, although the freestone tablet inscribed "A.T. 1673. A.D." was not placed, as originally over the arch, but built into the adjoining lower wall. The initials are those of Andrew Thomson, Advocate and Sheriff-Depute, and of his wife Agnes Divie; the date is later than the arch and probably refers to the additions made to the early 17th century house at this time. Andrew Thomson died 1690, and the property passed to Sir Alexander Bannerman of Elsick who was succeeded by his younger son Patrick Bannerman, the Jacobite Provost in 1715; he proclaimed and welcomed the Old Pretender as King James the 8th after his landing at Peterhead. Bannerman was later imprisoned at Carlisle, but made his escape to France.

In a nearby house, No. 15 Guestrow, built on what had been Bannerman property, Archibald Simpson, Architect, was born in 1790. A simple building with good interior plasterwork and panelling, it was designed about 1786 by Simpson's architect uncle - William Dauney.

Known also as the Powis Burn, now underground near King's College and the Aulton, this burn flowed into the Don's original channel south by way of the Links; it now runs north under the west edge of the King's Links to reach the Don. It was so-called because it passed the site of the Seaton Tile and Brick Works – Map Ref. 949086 – which, from the end of the 17th century, produced Scotch bricks and pantiles; the buildings were demolished in the 1920s. On grassland where the burn meets the river, and between it and the Esplanade stands a grey granite stone (Map Ref. 950092). This is the last boundary marker of the Inner and Outer Marches of the Royal Burgh of Aberdeen. Known as the "Omega" stone as it is inscribed with the last letter of the Greek alphabet, it also has the letters "ABD" – Aberdeen, and "C.R." for City Regality.

The Omega Stone.

At the highest part of Tillydrone Road, this prominent mound - Map Ref. 93660886 - is a Scheduled Ancient Monument; it dominated the Cathedral and the Chanonry precinct and overlooks the course of the River Don down below. The river here, until the late 18th century, flowed in a wide loop as far east as St. Machar's. Tillydrone, the name being Gaelic meaning "hillock on the ridge", was the site of the 12th century earthwork and timber castle of the early Bishops of Aberdeen. It also commanded the ancient north roadway, which, before Balgownie's Brig, crossed the Don by the ford, later a ferry, at the Cruives Dykes just upstream. The motte's oval summit, now only about 20ft. (6M.) across, due to erosion down the steep river bank, stands about 26ft. (8M.) above the surrounding ground to the east, and 49ft. (15M.) high on the west. After the Bishop's Palace near the Cathedral was built in the early 14th century Tillydrone continued as the locus for the bishops' open-air courts; it was sometimes called the hill of St. Thomas the Martyr (A'Becket) as a chapel dedicated to him once existed there.

Tillydrone Motehill

Tillydrone Port was the gateway to the Chanonry from the north-west, the site (Map Ref. 93720883) being near the motehill, with the Parson of Kinkell's Manse, built 1424, to the south. Also known as Market Port, it led to the Aulton's Market Stance - Map Ref. 090087 - where horse fairs and cattlemarkets were held on Skeir Thursday, the day before Good Friday. There was also the Aulton Market lasting 8 days in mid-October - its other name, St Luke's Fair being a corrupt form of Simmerluak's, or St Moluag's Fair. The last horse fair on the Market Stance, now built over with University buildings, was in 1933.

Dating mainly from 1615 and 1627, the builder being Thomas Watsoun, the Tolbooth is now incorporated behind the granite frontage of the 1868-74 Town House and Sheriff Courthouse in Castle Street. Aberdeen has had three tolbooths; the earliest is believed to have been sited near the quay from about 1191 till 1394 when King Robert 3rd granted a licence to the burgesses to build a town-house on the present location. The building, of early 17th century date, also called the High Tolbooth, is really like a strong towerhouse; it is rectangular in plan with four stone-vaulted storeys crowned by a parapet walk with open corner turrets, and the balustraded clock tower has a graceful lead spire. The old jail cells - known as the Mids o' Mar - retain their grim atmosphere; these dark confined vaults lit by wee barred windows are reached by narrow spiral stairs in the thick walls. To the prisoner' shackles and chains is added the security of heavy studded doors and iron yetts. The original pedimented entrance door and double forestairs to the Castlegate were unfortunately removed when the Victorian frontage was erected. Also demolished (1867) was the Laigh Tolbooth, adjoining on the west; this 3-storey building dating from 1730 - William Adam, Architect - had contained the council chamber and courts. A surviving feature from this building is the fine single-face metal sundial with Latin inscription: "Ut umbra sic vita fugit" - Like a shadow, life flies.

Tolbooth from Lodge Walk

Old Aberdeen became a free burgh of barony by King James 4th's charter of 1498, and almost 400 years later lost its burghal status when it was merged into Aberdeen City in 1891. At the north end of High Street is the excellent Georgian Town House built 1788 - George Jaffrey, Architect. Solid and symmetrical, it stands three storeys high under a piended slate roof with a central pediment and clock turret topped by a cupola. Over the entrance door is a freestone panel displaying the burgh coat-of-arms, dated 1721, with its Latin motto: "Concordia res parvae crescunt" - By harmony small things increase. This panel's date may refer to an earlier town house on the same site, along with another old stone, a dormer pediment with the Royal Arms, now built into the east wall. Although no longer used for burgh administration, the building has part of an old cell with door to be seen inside on the ground floor, and a wee barred jail window still exists on the east gable. Much of the original interior remains; the first floor, now a public library, has some old 17th century chairs carved with the emblems of the five Incorporated Trades of the Aulton - Hammermen, Tailors, Shoemakers, Weavers, Fleshers. At second floor a masonic lodge occupies what was the old burgh's council chamber with its coved ceiling.

Set back on the north side of Little Belmont Street, this classical building - erected to the design of John Smith in 1841 - is a particularly pleasing architectural composition in ashlar granite with a central entrance portico of four strong Greek Doric columns with pediment over, and flanked by two side wings. The gates and railings - now gone - were very good examples of cast-iron work. Known also as the Old High School, it later became part of the Central School (the old name of the Aberdeen Academy) and is still an educational building.

Tarnty Ha'

Also known as Mathurine or Red Friars, the Order of the Holy Trinity became established in Aberdeen before 1273; King William the Lyon, before his death (1214) is said to have granted the Trinitarians his royal residence and garden near the Green, at the foot of what is now Exchange Street - Map Ref. 94250605. However this royal "palace" - possibly a timber hall - still existed in 1332 when King David 2nd granted it to Sir John Somerville, so the Trinitarians may have occupied the building only until their conventual accommodation was built. Never a large or wealthy community, the friary continued till 1559 when it was burnt by the Protestants - a friar, Francis, died in the flames. In 1631 Dr. William Guild, (commemorated in Guild Street) bought and gifted to the Seven Incorporated Trades, the Trinitarians' medieval chapel, and also the late 16th century building which became the Trades Hall or Tarnty Ha' (Trinity Hall) - a two-storey L-plan structure containing a meeting hall about 67ft (20M.) long by 17ft (5M.) wide and 16ft (4.8M.) high. Its projecting wing tower with entrance door and corbelled angle turret was very similar to other contemporary buildings by the master-mason Andrew Jamesone. The Hall was extended in 1632 when the fine Renaissance arched gate with inscribed panels was built; both were demolished around 1857, when the arch was rebuilt in below the later 1846 Trinity Hall. The Trinity Chapel became an Episcopal church from 1703 till 1794, when it had become ruinous and was removed, to be replaced by a Chapel of Ease for Seceders. At the Disruption of 1843 this ceased as a church and by 1867 it became part of the old Alhambra Music Hall until 1902; it is now commercial premises - Nos. 12-14 Guild Street.

The seven Incorporated Trades - the Hammermen, Tailors, Fleshers Cordwainers, Baxters, Weavers, and Wrights and Coopers, - all established by 1534 - moved from old Tarnty Ha' to a new Hall built in 1846 at Nos. 151-155 Union Street; the architects were John Smith (1781-1852) and his son William (1817-1891). The architectural style is Tudor Gothic, not altogether in keeping with other Union Street frontages. Above shops at pavement level, the large hall occupied the first floor, and the basement at Lower Denburn level contained the Trades School entered through the rebuilt gateway of 1632; the moulded archway had above it three ornate panels with surrounds. On the left was the Guild family coat-of-arms and initials D.W.G. (Doctor William Guild) and FVNDATOR (Founder); the centre panel had the Royal Arms of Scotland and G.R. (Gulielmus Rex-King William) over two figurines holding a scroll reading: "TO.Y.GLORIE.OF.GOD.AND.COMFORT. OF.Y.POOR.THIS.HOWS.WAS.GIWEN.TO.Y. CRAFTS.BY.MR.WILLM.GVILD.DOCTOVR.OF. DIVINITIE.MINISTER.OF.ABD.1633", and above, in 16th century lettering, in Latin: "FVNDAVIT.GVLIELM.R.SCOT.1181" (Founded.William King of Scots.1181); surmounting this was an urn above the Latin motto: "SOLI DEO GLORIE" (To God alone the Glory) and date 1632. The right-hand panel was inscribed: "HE.THAT.PITIETH.THE.POORE.LENDETH.TO. THE.LORD.AND.THAT.WHICH.HE.HATH.GIVEN. WILL.HE.REPAY.PRO.19.17". In 1893 the whole archway was taken down, and while some fragments were preserved in the Hall, the 1181 inscription went missing although believed to be in a garden near Aberdeen.

The Trinity Hall building, no longer occupied by the Trades, became part of a shopping development (1964) - the Victorian Gothic hall with its timber ceiling was retained in a restaurant.

Trinity Hall Gateway · 1632-3

TRIPLE KIRKS

This architecturally interesting group of buildings in Schoolhill, originally three Free Kirks, was designed, in the Early Pointed Gothic style, by Archibald Simpson, Architect, after the Disruption of 1843. By using the cheapest materials building work was soon completed by 1844. The graceful tower and spire, a design similar to one of the twin spires of St Elizabeth Kirche, Marburg, West Germany, is unique as one of the few successful brickwork structures in the Granite City. Generally the walls are rubble granite masonry; string-courses and window rybats are sandstone, with brick pointed arches. The three churches were, from 1844, the Free East, the Free West and the Free South Kirks, becoming in the later 19th century the two Free Kirks, the East and the High, latterly the East and Belmont Church; and the Congregational Church of Albion and St Paul's. Now no longer in use for worship, the buildings are partially converted to commercial premises.

Cat Cairn and Consumption Dyke.

On Tullos Hill are four round stone burial cairns - Map Ref. 9503 - forming a Bronze Age cemetery dating from around 1500 B.C. All are Scheduled Ancient Monuments but none has as yet been excavated. Tullos Cairn - Map Ref. 959041 - is about 65ft (20M) across, and 10ft (3M) high; it is the most northerly of the group, located lower than the others on the ridge of the hill. About 500 yards (450M.) to the south stands Baron's Cairn on a high knoll, 274ft (83M.) above sea level; although much denuded of stones it is still some 60ft. (18M.) in diameter and about 5½ft. (1.7M.) high. Due east about 550 yards (500M.) is the smaller Crab's Cairn - much disturbed, now 46ft (14M.) across by 5ft. (1.5M.) high. At a distance of 875 yards (800M.) southwest of the Baron's Cairn stands the largest burial monument on the highest point of the hill; Cat Cairn is 72ft. (22M.) by 62ft (19M.) and about 13ft (4M.) high, and round the north and south sides may be the remains of an encircling shelf or platform. The three last-named cairns are on the line of the old southern boundary of the City of Aberdeen. Nearby are remnants of "consumption-dykes", 19th century field enclosure walls composed of stone gatherings.

Near a boggy howe between Tullos and Crab's Cairns is the site - Map Ref. 959039 - of Jacob's Well; its stone arch 1M. (3¼ft.) high is now at Duthie Park Winter Gardens. The heathery braes of Tullos Hill are still the haunt of roe as in medieval times when the Abbots of Arbroath hunted in their deer forest, but eastward the onetime farmparks of Ness are now an ugly devastation caused by uncontrolled rubbish tipping.

This historical landmark was situated on the Old Deeside Road on the section now known as Auchinyell Road along the high ground above the hollow of the Ruthrieston burn where ran the former Deeside Railway line. At Twa-Mile Cross – Map Ref. 913034 approximately – in September 1644 Montrose and his Royalist army encamped, after fording the River Dee at Drum. The Covenant forces, with Aberdeen's citizen levies marched out to confront him, but were later to be disastrously routed at the Battle of Aberdeen in the Hardgate and Justice Mills area.
All the fields of what was Garthdee Farm and the small-holding of Two-mile Cross, east of which an old roadway linked, before the railway, the old and the present Deeside roads, are now built up with housing. The naming of a street as Two Mile Cross, about 800M. (½ mile) to the south-east in the Kaimhill housing area confuses the identification of the true location of this historic spot which should surely be marked by a stone and descriptive tablet commemorating what was a notable event in the story of Aberdeen's past.

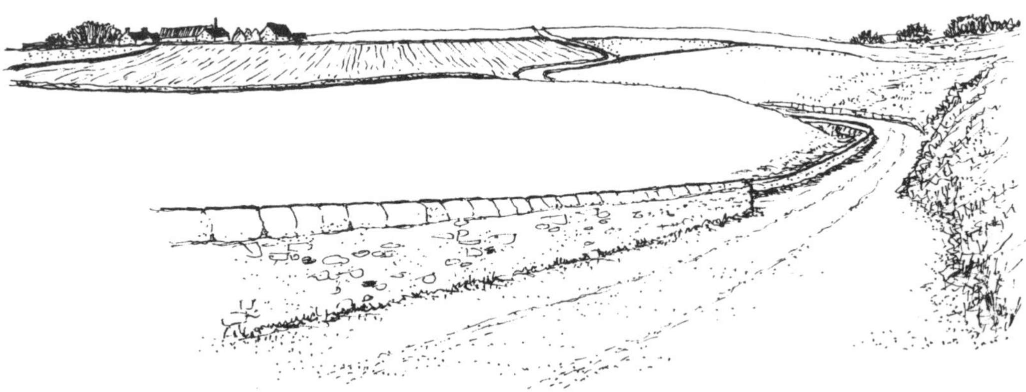

Old Deeside Road from Auchinyell around 1920: Twa-mile Cross was just beyond centre skyline.

Union Bridge – around 1850 – from the south-west.

The building of the city's principal thoroughfare, Union Street, which cut through the medieval burgh from east to west, followed on a report by Charles Abercrombie, Engineer, in 1796. From the Adelphi the approach to the crossing of the Denburn valley was carried on a series of arches begun in 1800 by Abercrombie and David Hamilton, a Glasgow architect. The original 3-arch design for Union Bridge by Hamilton was abandoned in favour of a single 132ft.(40M.) span proposed by the celebrated Scots engineer Thomas Telford. Begun in 1802 with William Ross as the builder, this handsome, well-proportioned example of bridge engineering with remarkably fine architectural detail was completed in 1805. A major change occurred when widening took place in 1907, but in 1964 the whole concept was virtually spoilt by the building of an ugly row of shops along the south side; this with further development obscures a once fine view to Torry and Tullos Hill on the southern horizon.

West of the Bridge along the rest of Union Street – named after the unsuccessful union of Britain and Ireland in 1800 – many of the buildings, either by Archibald Simpson, or in his style, adhered to a regular terraced facade of four storeys generally, built in good ashlar granite.

UNION CHAMBERS

Built in 1814 this was the first building in the town to be designed by Archibald Simpson, Architect. Now Nos. 46-50 Union Street, it was originally known as Morison of Auchintoul's house; the pend at No. 50 leads to McCombie's Court and the Netherkirkgate. The building is an interesting example of good street architecture. Union Chambers, four storeys high, has a central feature with four windows, the chimney-heads over each pair of windows forming a duality in the composition of the frontage. Architrave and cornice detailing is restrained and skilful, typical of much of Simpson's later designs using granite. The interior has been reconstructed and the third floor, with the street level shops, was altered in the late 19th century.

Known sometimes in the Middle Ages as the Overkirkgate, this is one of the city's oldest streets, first mentioned, in records, in 1382. It led from Broad Street to the north side of St Nicholas Kirk, which was outwith the burgh's ports. Although all the south side of the street was gone by 1954, some good buildings remain on the opposite side. Dating from 1694, the house at Nos. 24-26 is three storeys high; the asymmetrical frontage has deep-set windows with Gothic wave mouldings at lintels and jambs. Skewputts are unusually high and projecting on three courses of corbelling; both projections carrying sundials. The inside stair has a finely turned newel post and the ground floor is now a shop. On a wing at the back along Drum's Lane is a curved skew-corbel with the initials W.T. and the date 1718. At the east sundial on the street are the initials W.T.-M.G. and the date 1694. The original slated roof, with eaves gutter and ornamental leadwork rainwater heads, was removed about 1953, and the harling stripped off. Improvements in 1981 partially restored the late medieval character of this building, which is said to have been a provost's town-house in the 18th century.

Nos 24-26 Upperkirkgate

In 1806 at No. 4 Upperkirkgate, in Ross's Court, a bronze pot was unearthed during building operations, and was found to contain over 12,000 medieval coins, mostly English; the pot is now in Sir George Skene's Mansion, and some coins are at the Public Library.

UPPERKIRKGATE PORT

Nº 42 Upperkirkgate.

Dating from before 1443 this was the last of the medieval burgh's gateways to be removed; it was still standing in 1794. The Port stood near the foot of the Upperkirkgate. At its location-Map Ref. 94120641 - there was, until the whole south side of the street was removed about 1953, a deep set-back in the building line where the front of No. 41 projected into the old street; a small projection, still apparent, also occurs at No. 46 on the opposite side.

West of the port the Loch Burn, or Flourmill Burn, originally a defensive feature, flowed under the roadway. The close called Burn Court is a relic of the time when the watercourse was not underground.

Standing just within where the Port was, No. 42 Upperkirkgate is a 17th century three-storey house; its smooth rendered gable with high lum to the street make it one of the town's few remaining "gable-end" buildings. The windows have moulded surrounds formed of dressed sandstone, and the original interesting interior included timber panelling, fine plaster cornices and one good mantelpiece.

One of the most pleasing thoroughfares near the west end of Union Street, Victoria Street was named after Queen Victoria who reigned 1837-1901. Originally planned by Archibald Simpson, Architect, he designed the first houses to be built around 1843; these are Nos. 8-16 (on the west side), single-storey with rubble walls, and Nos. 18-56, also single-storey. There are pedimented doorways and higher wallheads at Nos. 34-42. On the east side, Nos. 21-39, two-storeyed terraced houses, were by Simpson (1843), also Nos. 7-11, although begun in 1849, two years after his death. Nos. 17 and 19 dated from about 1850, and Nos. 13 and 15 completed the whole scheme by around 1860. Although there are variations in design details, textures and finishes, and some later external alterations, nevertheless the general scale and good proportions make this a splendid example of a classic early Victorian street of terrace houses.

Located about 96M. (105 yards) northwest of the Skene Street end of Victoria Street is the site, on the east bank of the Denburn adjoining the Grammar School grounds, of Carden's Well - Map Ref. 93120613; this spring in 1706 became one source of the town's water supply from the area of Carden Haugh, until augmented by the Fountainhall cisterns. Another nearby well can still be seen, now underground in the back garden of Carden House School, and approached down a narrow flight of steps.

Water House
about 1850

Most of the Union Street frontages are of three storeys but this building (now Nos. 478-484 - originally No. 40 Union Place in early 19th century) is conspicuous in being four storeys high. Designed by City Architect John Smith in 1830, this unusual building has an ashlar granite frontage with pillars between first and third floors surmounted by a block pediment; it contained the reservoir for part of the town's water supply pumped from a well on the north bank of the Dee, upstream of the Bridge of Dee. It ceased to be the Water House after the completion of the Invercannie Waterworks in 1866, and became a fire station till 1872. Now used as offices and commercial premises, it was altered and reconstructed about 1900.

The western end of Union Street was mainly residential in the early nineteenth century, and notable features of the houses were the attractive railinged basements and entrance doors approached by steps. As the properties became converted to commercial uses, these, except at Nos. 222 and 224, were eventually removed to provide wider pavements.

This building, important in the medieval life and trading of the burgh, was situated where the Harbour Office building (1885) stands to-day on Regents Quay - Map Ref. 94440617. The Weigh-house, demolished in 1883, had been built in 1631 as a "Pack-house" or "Tron", where dues were paid for weighing and packing merchandise unloaded at the quays. It was a long plain building of two storeys with four dormer windows of the old sloping-roof type. Forestairs led up to a first floor balcony projecting along the frontage to the quay; the timbers from an Amsterdam galley wrecked on Belhelvie sands in 1707 are said to have formed the structure of this balcony. At the east gable was a flight of forestairs giving access to a back wing. To the north-east of the building is the open area still known as Weigh-house Square.

WELLINGTON SUSPENSION BRIDGE

The "Chain Briggie", very much an Aberdeen landmark, was built in 1831; it is a Scheduled Ancient Monument in the structural engineering category. In 1983 it was superseded, a short distance down-river, by a wider concrete bridge now carrying the road traffic. The Wellington Bridge replaced the old ferry passage between Torry and Ferryhill, hence the latter name. The bridge engineer was Sir Samuel Brown and the contractor was James Abernethy. John Smith, Architect, designed the approaches and the pylons, with their archways, at each end, the south pylon rising from the rocky outcrop of Craiglug. At the north side an arch, dated 1886, spans Riverside Drive under the north approach road, where stood, until demolition in the 1960s, an octagonal toll-house, also a design by John Smith.

Except for the cast-iron pillared veranda attached in Victorian times to the south front, this mansion in Westburn Park — one-storey with basement area on the north — stands as it was built by Archibald Simpson in 1836-9. The architectural effect of the central semi-circular projection on the south side is lost due to the veranda, but the house displays the architect's Neo-Grecian style as its most attractive. The west portico entrance with its four Greek Doric columns and pediment shows Simpson's originality in design of classical details. The walls are of stuccoed brickwork and the low-pitch roof is slated and piended with considerable eaves projection. The House was built for David Chalmers, printer and grandson of James Chalmers, the founder of the "Aberdeen Journal". The property, known as West Burn of Rubislaw, belonged in 1810 to ex-Provost George More of Raeden; a house had existed here prior to 1820. The surrounding Westburn Park dates from after the Town Council's acquisition of the House and grounds in 1899. Repairs and renovation work were carried out in 1954, but some of the building's original fine interior decoration remains.

The rebuilt Windmill at Drumgarth.

A windmill existed in Aberdeen as early as 1270 but its location is not known. Another stood at the head of the Gallowgate on Windmillhill, later called the Porthill; it was built about 1602 and existed (Map Ref. 9413 0684) throughout the 17th century. Near Windmill Brae was the site of a later mill, which was built before 1680 and stood at Windmill Lane – Map Ref. 93900594 – until the mid-19th century. Then it was demolished and partly rebuilt at a new location, as a "garden-house" in the grounds of Drumgarth, Pitfodels, a large mansion built by George Jameson, jeweller, in 1859; this date, with monograms, including G.I., is inserted over the door of the circular building. The original inscribed lintel has the date 1680; the weathervane, on top of the conical slated roof, has the letters ABDN for Aberdeen and the later date · 1760.

WOODHILL HOUSE

Woodhill House was probably erected after 1780 when the lands were feued by John Gordon of Craig who died in 1800, being succeeded by his son James who died 1852. Demolished in 1975 to make way for local authority offices, it stood in pleasant wooded grounds - Map Ref. 912069, and was an attractive two-storey Georgian mansion-house, the central block having stuccoed walls and a low-pitched slated roof; the entrance portico had Roman Doric columns. The flanking single-storey pavilion wings were enhanced by windows set in semi-circular arched recesses.

Situated on the wooded south bank of the River Don and approached by a driveway from Mugiemoss Road, the oldest part of Woodside House, dating from 1769 when the estate of Old Cruives was owned by Patrick Barron, is a two-storeyed rubble granite building attached to the north of the later house of around 1840. Barron's son, also Patrick, was a partner in the cotton-mill firm of Gordon Barron and Co., founded before 1785. The present mansion of ashlar granite was built by George Elmsly; it faces south with a recessed entrance portion and Roman Doric columned porch. There are bay windows at east and west gables and the piended slate roof has overhanging eaves. The building is now used as office accommodation.

Some 300 yards (270M.) to the west and above the steep, picturesque tree-clad bank of the river at the bend known as Old Cruives, is the semi-ruinous structure called "The Barracks". It's design is in the pseudo-Gothic castellated style and it dates from the unhappy times before 1800 when child-labourers employed by the cotton millowners were lodged here.

"The Barracks"

Woodside, a small village dating from the 15th century, became a police burgh in 1868; its community of granite quarriers and millworkers was absorbed into the city in 1891. Of its churches the most interesting is the South Kirk in Church Street. Designed by Archibald Simpson, Architect, it was built 1846-9 in a Classical Italianate style, with rubble masonry walls under wide projecting eaves. The windows have semi-circular arched heads, similar in design to those at Simpson's other, plainer Woodside church, now the North, but originally the Parish Kirk when built (1836), becoming a Free Church at the 1843 Disruption. The dominant feature of the South Kirk is the handsome north tower, a vertical landmark in Woodside; octagonal in plan, built of coursed dressed granite and surmounted by a circular cupola above the clock, with its four faces, dating from 1867.

WRIGHTS AND COOPERS PLACE

This short lane, off the east side of Old Aberdeen's High Street, is a notable example of the sympathetic conservation of old Scottish domestic architecture; restoration architects were Robert Hurd and Partners, Edinburgh, in 1965. The linked houses, dating from the 18th century and the early 1800s, are all two-storeyed; Nos. 1 and 2, and No. 5 having slated roofs, Nos. 3 and 4, red pantiles. Except for No. 3, with its rendered walls, the houses have the traditional granite rubble masonry exposed; No. 5 - originally No. 9 - has been considerably rebuilt. The 20th century type of paving layout and the designed landscaping lacks the robust informality typical of the older Scots burgh townscape, but this little precinct gives a reasonably good impression of the Aulton as it was in the late 18th century.

ABERDEEN

What marvellous mad hopes were cherished
        In Aberdeen!
Oh, that's a city to be born in.
        The pure air kindles you, and witty
Your mind goes dancing. To learn scorn in
        Oh, that's a city.
Under the Crown that dreams of Flodden
        And Borgia, in scarlet gown
Youth lightly treads where Youth hath trodden
        Under the Crown.

Rachel Annand Taylor

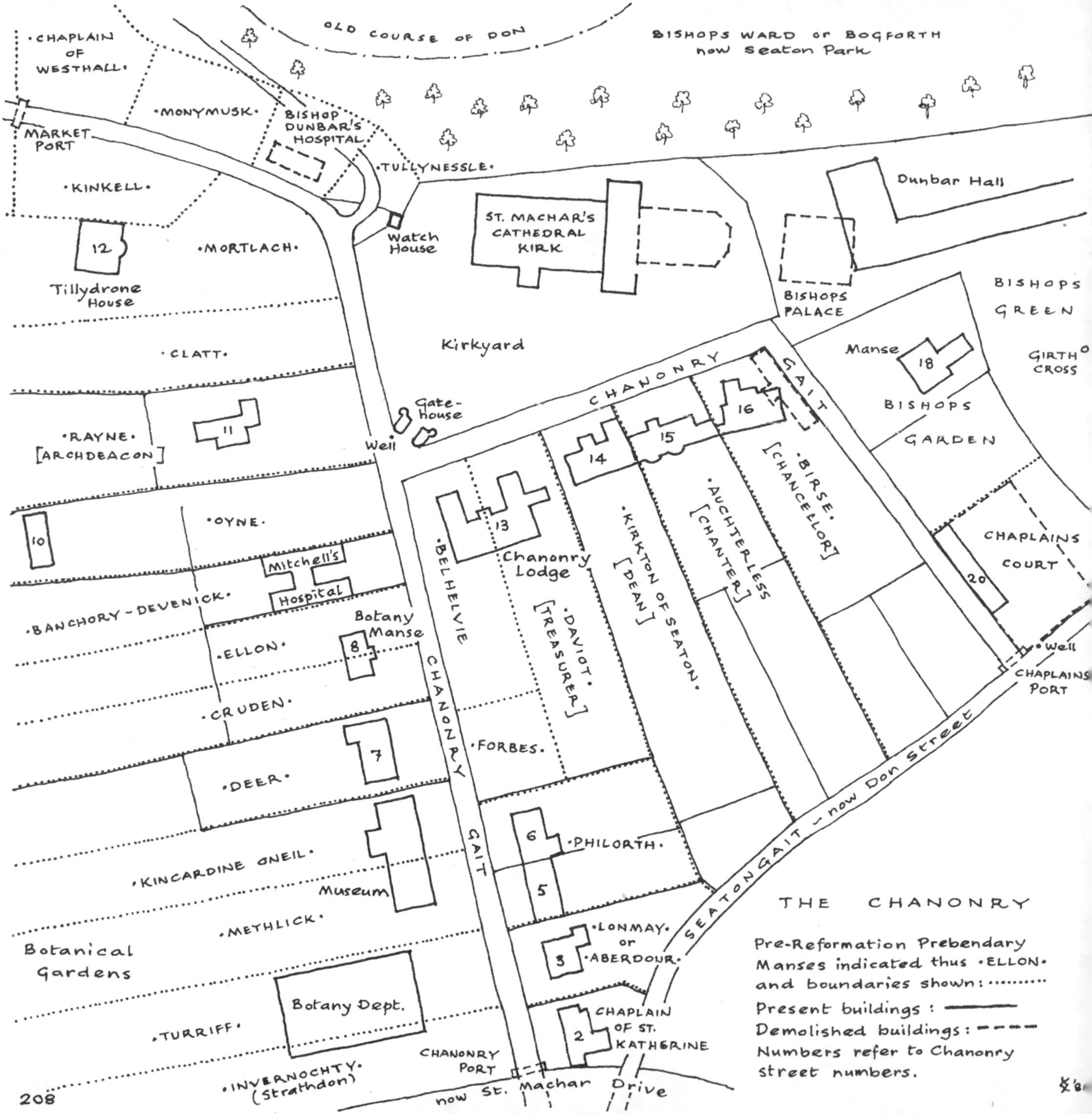

OLD COURSE OF DON
BISHOPS WARD or BOGFORTH now Seaton Park
CHAPLAIN OF WESTHALL
MONYMUSK
BISHOP DUNBAR'S HOSPITAL
MARKET PORT
KINKELL
TULLYNESSLE
Dunbar Hall
ST. MACHAR'S CATHEDRAL KIRK
Watch House
12
Tillydrone House
MORTLACH
BISHOPS PALACE
BISHOPS GREEN
Kirkyard
CLATT
CHANONRY
GAIT
Manse
18
GIRTH CROSS
Gate-house
Well
11
RAYNE
[ARCHDEACON]
14
15
16
BISHOPS GARDEN
BIRSE [CHANCELLOR]
AUCHTERLESS [CHANTER]
KIRKTON OF SEATON [DEAN]
10
OYNE
13
Chanonry Lodge
BELHELVIE
CHAPLAINS COURT
20
Mitchell's Hospital
BANCHORY-DEVENICK
Botany Manse
8
ELLON
DAVIOT [TREASURER]
CHANONRY
Well
CHAPLAINS PORT
CRUDEN
FORBES
7
DEER
SEATONGAIT – now Don Street
GAIT
6
PHILORTH
KINCARDINE ONEIL
Museum
5
METHLICK
LONMAY or ABERDOUR
3
Botanical Gardens
Botany Dept.
TURRIFF
2
CHAPLAIN OF ST. KATHERINE
CHANONRY PORT
INVERNOCHTY (Strathdon)
now St. Machar Drive
THE CHANONRY
Pre-Reformation Prebendary Manses indicated thus •ELLON• and boundaries shown: ....
Present buildings: ———
Demolished buildings: - - - -
Numbers refer to Chanonry street numbers.

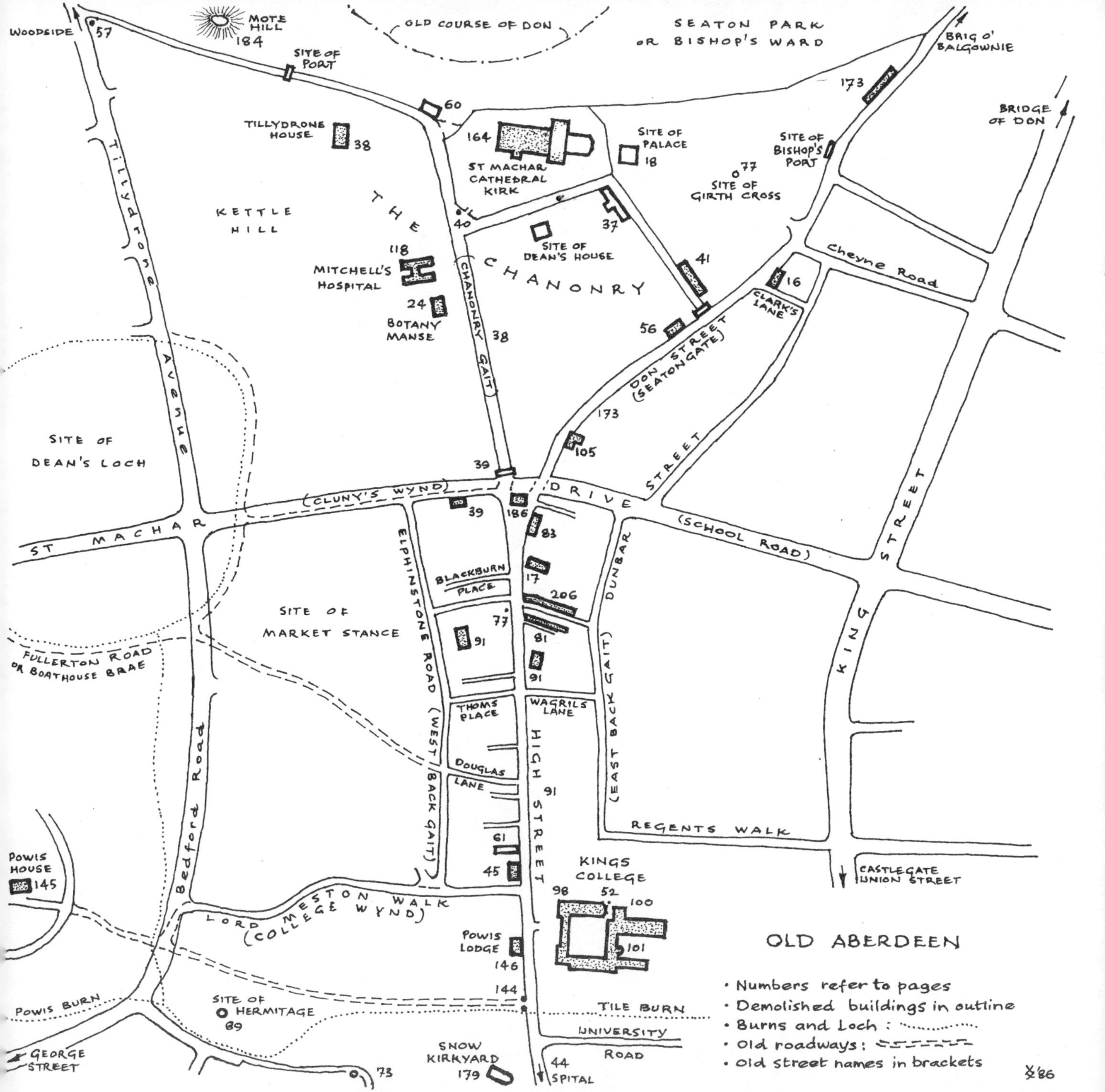

OLD ABERDEEN
• Numbers refer to pages
• Demolished buildings in outline
• Burns and Loch :
• Old roadways :
• Old street names in brackets
WOODSIDE 57
MOTE HILL 184
OLD COURSE OF DON
SEATON PARK OR BISHOP'S WARD
BRIG O' BALGOWNIE
SITE OF PORT
60
173
TILLYDRONE HOUSE 38
164
ST MACHAR CATHEDRAL KIRK
SITE OF PALACE 18
SITE OF BISHOP'S PORT
BRIDGE OF DON
77 SITE OF GIRTH CROSS
KETTLE HILL
THE CHANONRY
40
SITE OF DEAN'S HOUSE
37
41
Cheyne Road
118 MITCHELL'S HOSPITAL
24 BOTANY MANSE
CHANONRY GAIT 38
16
CLARK'S LANE
56
DON STREET (SEATON GATE)
173
105
SITE OF DEAN'S LOCH
Tillydrone Avenue
39
(CLUNY'S WYND)
DRIVE
STREET
ST MACHAR
39 186 83
(SCHOOL ROAD)
KING STREET
BLACKBURN PLACE
17
206
DUNBAR
SITE OF MARKET STANCE
77
91
81
91
FULLERTON ROAD OR BOATHOUSE BRAE
ELPHINSTONE ROAD (WEST BACK GAIT)
THOMS PLACE
WAGRILS LANE
(EAST BACK GAIT)
DOUGLAS LANE
HIGH STREET 91
REGENTS WALK
Bedford Road
61
45
POWIS HOUSE 145
KINGS COLLEGE
98 52 100
101
CASTLEGATE UNION STREET
LORD MESTON WALK (COLLEGE WYND)
POWIS LODGE 146
144
POWIS BURN
SITE OF HERMITAGE 89
TILE BURN
UNIVERSITY ROAD
GEORGE STREET
73
SNOW KIRKYARD 179
44 SPITAL